ECLIPSE INTERPRETATION MANUAL

by

ROSE LINEMAN

First Printing: 1986
Third Printing 1993

ISBN: 0-86690-301-1
Library of Congress Catalog Card No.: 85-71468

Published by:
American Federation of Astrologers, Inc.
PO Box 22040
6535 S. Rural Road
Tempe, AZ 85285-2040

Printed in the United States of America

DEDICATION

To the **American Federation of Astrologers**
and the principles for which it stands.

CONTENTS

CONTENTS

ACKNOWLEDGEMENT

To **Karen Ledney**,

my sincere thanks for invaluable technical assistance,

without which this book would have taken months,

perhaps years, longer to complete.

Rose Lineman

INTRODUCTION

Eclipses have long roused human curiosity and inspired scientific study. The mysteries they pose are not yet completely solved. Speculation continues as to their exact role in nature's scheme and their significance to life on Earth. Until recently, it was generally accepted by astrologers that no lunar eclipse occurred unless in sequence with a solar eclipse but that solar eclipses could and often did occur without a companion lunar eclipse. It is now known that each solar eclipse - total, annular or partial - is accompanied within two weeks before or after its appearance by at least one lunar eclipse - total, partial or penumbral (appulse) - and vice versa. Most eclipse sequences contain two eclipses, one lunar and one solar (not necessarily in that order), but because of Saros series overlaps, a sequence may contain three eclipses, two solar and one lunar or two lunar and one solar.

The fact of eclipse sequences puts new light on eclipse interpretation. Solar and lunar eclipses must be viewed as parts of a sequence which constitute a whole rather than as separate entities. One must consider the astrological relationship existing between the two or three eclipses of which a sequence is composed and the combined influence constituent eclipses exert in a natal horoscope. A sequence in which member eclipses fall in opposite signs of the zodiac has a different interpretational orientation than one in which member eclipses fall five signs apart. The interpretational slant of a sequence that is led off by a lunar eclipse differs from that of one led off by a solar eclipse. This book explores the astrological implications of eclipse sequences and the meanings of individual eclipses in relation to other eclipses of the same sequence.

Eclipse sequences explain why some eclipses remain active in a horoscope much longer than the traditional six-month period of influence. If any member of an eclipse sequence is aspected by a member of the succeeding sequence, the effective period of the earlier sequence is extended for another six months. It is not necessary that lunar eclipses aspect lunar eclipses and solar eclipses aspect solar eclipses to prolong eclipse sequence activity, only that one member of a particular eclipse sequence be aspected by either a lunar or solar eclipse belonging to the sequence immediately following. An aspect to any member of a sequence reactivates the entire sequence. Continued reactivation is possible indefinitely as long as one member eclipse from each *consecutive* eclipse sequence aspects a member of the sequence of interest. An extended period of eclipse activity creates dual influences in the horosocope, that of the prolonged sequence and that of the current one. In such instances, interpretation is based upon the interrelationships among all eclipses belonging to active sequences and their combined influence in the natal chart.

Interpretational theory introduced in my book *Eclipses: Astrological Guideposts* (American Federation of Astrologers, 1984) is enlarged upon and developed in detail in this book. Here, individual meanings of solar and lunar eclipses in the signs of the zodiac and houses of the natal horoscope and their aspects are presented along with techniques to adapt these interpretations according to sequence arrangement.

CHAPTER 1

SOLAR ECLIPSES IN THE SIGNS

Various factors which are not part of traditional natal delineation enter into eclipse interpretation, among them Saros series influence. The sign in which a solar eclipse occurs operates in conjunction with the sign of the initial eclipse in the Saros series to which that particular solar eclipse belongs.

The thirty-eight identified Saros series, numbered consecutively 1-19 at each of the Moon's nodes (north followed by south) observe a particular pattern of appearance. At six-month intervals, a solar eclipse belonging to a North Node series ("N") is followed by a corresponding (same series number) South Node ("S") solar eclipse which is followed by one from the succeeding (next highest series number) "N" series followed by its corresponding "S" solar eclipse and so on until one solar eclipse from each series at both nodes has made an appearance in proper sequence. The cycle then repeats. Anomalies occur when a replacement Saros series starts before the earlier one ends. During the period in which such a dual series operates, a triple sequence consisting of a solar eclipse followed by a lunar eclipse followed by second solar eclipse occurs. The two solar eclipses which occur one lunation cycle apart bear the same series number and nodal designation, the first belonging to the earlier starting series and the second to the replacement series. They are separated at mid-lunation cycle by a lunar eclipse of the same series number at the opposite node. The regular Saros series pattern resumes six months later with a solar eclipse from the following series.

INFLUENCE OF INITIAL SOLAR ECLIPSES

The influence an initial Saros series solar eclipse bears upon other eclipses belonging to that series compares to the influence the rising sign exerts upon other elements of a horoscope. In determining the significance of an initial eclipse, consider the decan and duad it occupies as well as natural sign characteristics. The first decan (0 degrees - 10 degrees) of a sign is sub-ruled by that sign's planetary ruler; the second decan (10 degrees - 20 degrees) is sub-ruled by the planetary ruler of the succeeding sign belonging to the same triplicity (air, earth, fire or water); the third decan (20 degrees - 30 degrees) is sub-ruled by the planetary ruler of the remaining member of that triplicity. Each of the twelve duads in a sign consists of 2-1/2 degrees. Duad sub-rulerships follow the natural order of the signs beginning with the planetary ruler of the sign of interest as sub-ruler of the first duad (1 degree - 2-1/2 degrees) and ending with the planetary ruler of the preceding sign as sub-ruler of the final (twelfth) duad (27-1/2 degrees - 30 degrees). Sub-rulers within a sign lend something of their own qualities to the degrees they influence as expressed in the context of natural sign expression.

1-N Saros Series: 13 degrees Capricorn. In the second decan (sub-ruled by Venus) and sixth duad (sub-ruled by Mercury) of Capricorn (ruled by Saturn), the initial eclipse of the 1-N series lends undertones of worldly ambition, materialism and common sense to sign expression of other eclipses belonging to this series. Its influence is more prominent in signs which share similar natural characteristics and, to a lesser degree, in the Saturn, Venus/Taurus and Mercury/Gemini decans or duads of other signs. A solar eclipse from this north node series is followed in about six months by one from the 1-S series.

1-S Saros Series: 29 degrees Leo. This initial eclipse in the third decan (sub-ruled by Mars) and twelfth duad (sub-ruled by the Moon) of Leo (ruled by the Sun) supplements natural power drives and self-confidence as expressed through the signs of solar eclipses belonging to this south node series. It adds a touch of boldness to series expression which, because of the Moon's influence in the twelfth duad, lacks much of the arrogance common to the third decan. At present (1984), the slowly moving fixed star

Regulus (29 degrees 36' Leo), in exact conjunction with this initial eclipse, emphasizes its impact. Fixed star influence upon this initial eclipse extends from approximately 1870 through 2012. A solar eclipse from this series is followed in about six months by one belonging to the 2-N series.

2-N Early Saros Series: 6 degrees Cancer. Until 1928 when its replacement series began, the 2-N early series operated as a single series. Thereafter, and until the year 2024 when it ends, 2-N operates as a dual series; an appearance of a solar eclipse belonging to the earlier 2-N series will be followed in about a month by one from the 1928 2-N replacement series. The 6 degrees Cancer initial eclipse applies only to the earlier series. In the first decan (ruled and sub-ruled by the Moon) and third duad (sub-ruled by Mercury) of Cancer, it combines emotional and intellectual responsiveness. Its influence is very subtle as it tends to absorb the coloring of the sign in which eclipses belonging to its series occur, changing expression to accommodate the sign a member eclipse occupies.

2-N Replacement Saros Series: 26 degrees Gemini. The combined influence of Mercury (ruler of Gemini) Uranus (third decan sub-ruler) and Mars (eleventh duad sub-ruler) in this initial eclipse flavors series sign expression with intellectual incentive, spontaneity and versatility. A solar eclipse from the 2-N replacement series is followed in about six months by one from the 2-S series.

2-S Saros Series: 2 degrees Taurus. The Taurean qualities of Venus which is sole ruler of the first decan and first duad of Taurus in which this initial eclipse occurred, provide a strongly fixed foundation for sign expression of eclipses belonging to this south node series. Initial eclipse influence here adds stability and endurance, qualities helpful to signs that lack them but which may produce obstinacy and/or dogmatism in signs that are predominantly similar. A solar eclipse from this series is followed in about six months by one belonging to the 3-N series.

3-N Saros Series: 22 degrees Libra. Venusian qualities as expressed in Libra (Venus, ruler of Libra) combine with Mercurian characteristics as expressed in Gemini (Mercury/Gemini sub-ruler of the third decan and ninth duad of Libra) in this initial eclipse to influence artistic intellectual expression and harmony in eclipses of the series. Protective qualities of the benefic fixed star Spica (at 23 degrees 37' Libra in 1984) were reflected in series activity during the nineteenth century and most of the first half of the twentieth when the star moved into exact conjunction with this initial eclipse. A solar eclipse from this series is followed in about six months by one belonging to the 3-S series.

3-S Saros Series: 27 degrees Leo. This change of duad accounts for variations between the influence of this initial eclipse and that of the 1-S series which appeared in 29 degrees Leo. Though confident and assertive, expression here is more verbal because of Mercury's sub-rulership of the eleventh duad and less sensitive without the Moon's influence (twelfth duad). Refer to the 1-S Saros series paragraph noting that Regulus moved out of conjunction with this initial eclipse about 1870. A solar eclipse from this series is followed in about six months by one belonging to the 4-N series.

4-N Saros Series: 11 degrees Gemini. The attractiveness and beauty of Venus (sub-ruler of the second decan and fifth duad of Gemini) as reflected in Libra adds greater charm to traditional Gemini qualities in this initial eclipse. Its influence softens harsh sign characteristics of eclipses belonging to the series and reinforces pleasing attributes and intellectual traits. A solar eclipse from this series is followed in about six months by one belonging to the 4-S series.

4-S Saros Series: 27 degrees Aries. Optimism and innovation promote the dynamic qualities of Aries (ruled by Mars) in the third decan (sub-ruled by Jupiter) and eleventh duad (sub-ruled by Uranus) in which the 4-S initial eclipse took place. Its influence energizes sign expression of eclipses belonging to the series, stressing incentive and action. A solar eclipse from this series is followed in about six months by one from the 5-N series.

5-N Saros Series: 19 degrees Libra. This initial eclipse in the second decan (sub-ruled by Uranus) and eighth duad (sub-ruled by Venus as expressed in Taurus) adds refreshing accents of fair play and social concern to sign expression of eclipses belonging to this series. It also reinforces any materialistic qualities naturally present in signs of member eclipses. A solar eclipse from this series is followed in about six months by one from the 5-S series.

5-S Early Saros Series. The initial eclipse of this series which ended in 1931 remains unidentified. Since 1784 when its replacement series began, a solar eclipse from this early series was followed in about one month by one from its replacement series.

5-S Replacement Saros Series: 22 degrees Cancer. From its beginning in 1784 and until 1931, this series operated as part of a dual series. Since 1931 it has followed a normal Saros pattern. Its initial eclipse carries marked Neptunian influence since both the third decan and ninth duad of Cancer (ruled by the Moon) are sub-ruled by Neptune. In this series, initial eclipse influence heightens sensitivity and reinforces psychic tendencies. During the years (approximately 1842 - 1985) when this initial eclipse exactly conjuncts the fixed star Pollux (at 22 degrees 59' Cancer in 1984), sign expression of member eclipses may take on subtle malicious undertones. A solar eclipse belonging to this series is followed in about six months by one from the 6-N series.

6-N Saros Series: 28 degrees Taurus. The cautious, disciplined expression associated with the third decan (sub-ruled by Saturn) of Taurus (ruled by Venus) displays touches of initiative in the twelfth duad in which this initial eclipse occurred because of Mars' influence as duad sub-ruler. During the nineteenth century and early part of the twentieth when the fixed star Alcyone (at 29 degrees 46' Taurus in 1984) exactly conjuncted this initial eclipse, sign expression of solar eclipses in the series contained a karmic nuance. About six months after the occurrence of a solar eclipse from this series, one from the 6-S series appears.

6-S Saros Series: 22 degrees Pisces. This initial eclipse in the third decan and ninth duad (both sub-ruled by Pluto) of Pisces (ruled by Neptune) reinforces covert tendencies in the signs in which member eclipses fall and subdues or subverts more overt characteristics. In a highly evolved chart, sign expression may be channeled along spiritual lines. A solar eclipse from the 7-N series follows one from this series in about six months.

7-N Saros Series: 17 degrees Libra. The influence of this initial eclipse, though similar to that of the 5-N series which occurred in the same decan (second, sub-ruled by Uranus) of Libra (ruled by Venus), lends to more dynamic expression since it appeared in the seventh duad (sub-ruled by Mars) rather than in the eighth (sub-ruled by Venus). Here, Uranus and Mars lend novelty and impetus to Libran expression. Initial eclipse influence harmonizes and unifies sign expression of member eclipses without dulling or stultifying natural sparkle and incentive. A solar eclipse from this series is followed in about six months by one belonging to the 7-S series.

7-S Saros Series 7 degrees Cancer. This initial eclipse is interpreted the same as that of the 2-N early Saros series which occurred in 6 degrees Cancer, both initial eclipses occupying the same decan (first, sub-ruled by the Moon), and duad (third, sub-ruled by Mercury) of Cancer (ruled by the Moon). Refer to the 2-N early Saros series paragraph. A solar eclipse belonging to this series is followed in about six months by one from the 8-N series.

8-N Saros Series: 6 degrees Gemini. Sign expression of eclipses belonging to this series reflects the intellectual vitality generated by its initial eclipse which occurred in the first decan (ruled and sub-ruled by Mercury) and third duad (sub-ruled by the Sun) of Gemini. Here, Mercury emphasizes and the Sun energizes natural mental affinities associated with the sign of interest. A solar eclipse from this series is followed in about six months by one from the 8-S series.

8-S Saros Series: 11 degrees Aries. The Sun, sub-ruler of both the second decan and fifth duad of Aries (ruled by Mars) in which this initial eclipse appeared strengthens natural Arian qualities. Initial eclipse influence is to vitalize; it promotes dynamic expression in signs of member eclipses. A solar eclipse from this series is followed in about six months by one from the 9-N series.

9-N Early Saros Series: 17 degrees Leo. From 1664 when the 9-N replacement series started until 1935 when this part of the dual series ended, a solar eclipse belonging to this earlier series was followed in about one month by one from the replacement series. Sign expression of solar eclipses belonging to the early series filters through the warmth, abundant vitality and animation symbolic of the second decan (sub-ruled by Jupiter) and seventh duad (sub-ruled by Uranus) of Leo (ruled by the Sun) in which this initial eclipse appeared.

9-N Replacement Saros Series: 28 degrees Leo. Initial eclipse influence in this series is basically the same as that of the 1-S Saros series which occurred in the same decan (third, sub-ruled by Mars) and duad (twelfth, sub-ruled by the Moon) of Leo (ruled by the Sun). However, influence of the fixed star Regulus in this initial eclipse was emphasized throughout the nineteenth century and until the early 1940's. Refer to the 1-S Saros series paragraph. A solar eclipse from this series is followed in about six months by one belonging to the 9-S series.

9-S Early Saros Series: 5 degrees Cancer. From 1917 when the 9-S replacement series began until 1971 when this earlier series ended, it operated as a dual series. During that period a solar eclipse belonging to the 9-S early series was followed in about a month by one from the 9-S replacement series. Prior to 1917, the early series was followed in about six months by a solar eclipse from the 10-N series according to the normal Saros pattern. For interpretation of initial eclipse influence in this series, read the paragraph for the 2-N early Saros series whose initial eclipse occurred in the same decan (first, sub-ruled by the Moon) and duad (third, sub-ruled by Mercury) of Cancer (ruled by the Moon).

9-S Replacement Saros Series: 26 degrees Cancer. This series operated as a dual series from its beginning in 1917 until 1971 when the earlier 2-S series ended; thereafter, it operates as a single series. In the third decan (sub-ruled by Neptune) and eleventh duad (sub-ruled by Venus as ruler of Taurus) of Cancer (ruled by the Moon), this initial eclipse adds sentiment and feeling to sign expression of member eclipses. During the years from about 1943 to 2086 when an exact conjunction with the fixed star Procyon (at 25 degrees 34' Cancer in 1984) operates, negative or unfortunate sign tendencies may manifest. A solar eclipse from this series is followed in about six months by one from the 10-N series.

10-N Saros Series: 10 degrees Taurus. The combination of earth qualities associated with Venus and Mercury as reflected in the second decan and fifth duad (both sub-ruled by Mercury as expressed in Virgo) of Taurus (ruled by Venus) in which this initial eclipse occurred shades sign expression of solar eclipses belonging to this series. Influence here is both practical and discriminating. A solar eclipse from this series is followed in about six months by one from the 10-S series.

10-S Saros Series: 26 degrees Pisces. This initial eclipse in the third decan (sub-ruled by Pluto) and eleventh duad (sub-ruled by Saturn) of Pisces (ruled by Neptune) acts to subtly undermine, restrain and/or weaken natural sign expression of member eclipses except those that appear in Pisces or signs compatible with Pisces or in a Saturn, Neptune or Pluto decan or duad of other signs. A solar eclipse from this series is followed in about six months by one belonging to the 11-N series.

11-N Saros Series: 16 degrees Leo. For interpretation of this initial eclipse refer to the 9-N early Saros series whose initial eclipse appeared in the same decan (second, sub-ruled by Jupiter) and duad (seventh, sub-ruled by Uranus) of Leo (ruled by the Sun). A solar eclipse from this series is followed in about six months by one from the 11-S series.

11-S Saros Series: 29 degrees Gemini. Sign expression of solar eclipses belonging to the 11-S series displays nuances of the whimsy and intellectual artistry symbolic of the third decan (sub-ruled by Uranus) and twelfth duad (sub-ruled by Venus) of Gemini (ruled by Mercury) in which its initial eclipse occurred. A solar eclipse from this series is followed in about six months by one from the 12-N series.

12-N Saros Series: 28 degrees Taurus. Read the paragraph for the 6-N Saros series whose initial eclipse occurred in the same degree of Taurus as this one. A solar eclipse belonging to this series is followed in about six months by one from the 12-S series.

12-S Early Saros Series: 6 degrees Libra. For most of the nineteenth century (after February 1812) this early series operated as part of a dual series. Only one solar eclipse from the series, its final eclipse, appeared in the twentieth century and that in April 1902. It was followed in about one month by a solar eclipse from its replacement series; for the remainder of the century, the replacement series continues as a single series. The influence of the first decan (sub-ruled by Venus) and the third duad (sub-ruled by Jupiter) of Libra (ruled by Venus) in which the initial eclipse of the earlier 12-S series appeared is to harmonize and relax, perhaps to the point of indolence in combination with a weak sign.

12-S Replacement Saros Series: 23 degrees Aquarius. In the third decan (sub-ruled by Venus) and tenth duad (sub-ruled by Pluto) of Aquarius (ruled by Uranus), this initial eclipse adds a provocative, sensual touch to sign expression of solar eclipses belonging to the 12-S replacement series. Its exact conjunction with the fixed star Deneb Algedi (at 23 degrees 19' Aquarius in 1984) lends to integrity of sign expression during the years from about 1890 to 2033. A solar eclipse from this series is followed in about six months by one belonging to the 13-N series.

13-N Saros Series: 21 degrees Leo. The third decan and ninth duad (both sub-ruled by Mars) of Leo (ruled by the Sun) in which this initial eclipse took place emphasizes fiery characteristics of the sign. Sign expression of solar eclipses belonging to the 13-N series reflects some of the spirited, animated qualities of the initial eclipse. A solar eclipse from this series is followed in about six months by one from the 13-S series.

13-S Saros Series: 6 degrees Gemini. The initial eclipse of this South Node series occurred in the same degree of Gemini as that of the 8-N series. For interpretation, refer to the 8-N Saros series paragraph. A solar eclipse from the 13-S series is followed in about six months by one belonging to the 14-N series.

14-N Saros Series: 15 degrees Taurus. The combined influence of Pluto (sub-ruler of the seventh duad) and Venus (ruler of Taurus) adds subtle sensuality to the practicality and orderliness symbolic of the second decan (sub-ruled by Mercury/Virgo) in which this initial eclipse appeared and which pervades sign expression of solar eclipses belonging to the 14-N series. A solar eclipse from this series is followed in about six months by one from the 14-S series.

14-S Saros Series: 10 degrees Virgo. The double influence of Saturn (sub-ruler of both the second decan and fifth duad of Virgo) emphasizes the methodical, business-like qualities of Virgo (ruled by Mercury) in this initial eclipse. Its influence in signs of member eclipses is to modify impulsive expression and to promote caution and conservativism. A solar eclipse belonging to the 14-S series is followed in about six months by one from the 15-N series.

15N-Saros Series: 27 degrees Cancer. For interpretation of this initial eclipse read the paragraph for the 9-S replacement Saros series whose initial eclipse in 26 degrees

Cancer appeared in the same decan and duad as this one. Disregard references to Procyon unless you are working with the twenty-first century since the fixed star does not move into orb of conjunction with the 15-N initial eclipse until approximately 2015. A solar eclipse from the 15-N series is followed in about six months by one belonging to the 15-S series.

15-S Saros Series: 24 degrees Gemini. With the initial eclipse in the third decan (sub-ruled by Uranus) and tenth duad (sub-ruled by Neptune) of Gemini (ruled by Mercury), sign expression of solar eclipses belonging to the 15-S series reflect spontaneous intellectual sensitivity. A solar eclipse from this series is followed in about six months by one from the 16-N series.

16-N Saros Series: 6 degrees Pisces. Signs of solar eclipses belonging to this series are expressed with an aura of romantic mystique and sensitivity symbolic of the first decan (ruled and sub-ruled by Neptune) and third duad (sub-ruled by Venus) of Pisces in which this initial eclipse appeared. A solar eclipse from this series is followed in about six months by one from the 16-S series.

16-S Saros Series: 28 degrees Virgo. This initial eclipse in the third decan (sub-ruled by Venus) and twelfth duad (sub-ruled by the Sun) of Virgo (ruled by Mercury) promotes expression that is practical, detailed and somewhat more vigorous than that usually attributed to Virgo. A solar eclipse from this series is followed in about six months by one from the 17-N series.

17-N Early Saros Series: 12 degrees Cancer. Emotional sensitivity and insight are heightened in the second decan and fifth duad (both sub-ruled by Pluto) of Cancer (ruled by the Moon) in which this initial eclipse occurred. Sign expression of member eclipses takes on psychic undertones. Prior to 1870 this series operated as a single series; thereafter and until it ended in 1942, it operated as part of a dual series, and a solar eclipse belonging to it was followed about a month after by one from the 17-N replacement series.

17-N Replacement Saros Series: 5 degrees Leo. Sign expression of solar eclipses belonging to this series exhibits touches of vitality and warmth symbolic of the first decan (ruled and sub-ruled by the Sun) and third duad (sub-ruled by Venus) of Leo in which this initial eclipse appeared in 1870. A solar eclipse from this series is followed in about six months by one from the 17-S series.

17-S Saros Series: 11 degrees Gemini. This initial eclipse, in the second decan and fifth duad (both sub-ruled by Venus) of Gemini (ruled by Mercury), occurred in the same degree of that sign as did the solar eclipse that initiated the 4-N Saros series. Refer to that paragraph for interpretation. A solar eclipse from this series is followed in about six months by one belonging to the 18-N series.

18-N Saros Series: 21 degrees Aquarius. Sign expression of solar eclipses belonging to this series contains an essence of human concern and social justice characteristic of its initial eclipse which appeared in the third decan and ninth duad (both sub-ruled by Venus as reflected in Libra) of Aquarius (ruled by Uranus). An 18-N solar eclipse is followed in about six months by one from the 18-S series.

18-S Saros Series: 3 degrees Virgo. In the first decan (ruled and sub-ruled by Mercury) and second duad (sub-ruled by Venus/Libra) of Virgo, this initial eclipse lends to sign expression of member eclipses nuances of fastidiousness and refinement. A solar eclipse belonging to this series is followed in about six months by one from the 19-N series.

19-N Saros Series: 21 degrees Cancer. The influence of this initial eclipse in the third decan and ninth duad (both sub-ruled by Neptune) of Cancer (ruled by the Moon) is emotional and esoteric; psychic and/or spiritual sensitivity colors sign expression of eclipses belonging to the series. A solar eclipse from the 19-N series is followed in about six months by one from the 19-S series.

19-S Saros Series. The initial eclipse of this series remains unidentified. A solar eclipse from the 19-S series completes the eighteen year (approximate) cycle of Saros series; it is followed in about six months by one from the 1-N series which begins another cycle.

SIGN EXPRESSION OF SOLAR ECLIPSES

The sign that a transiting solar eclipse occupies characterizes the manner by which eclipse activity is expressed. Direction of action depends upon the houses occupied and influenced by the eclipse; quality of action depends upon the aspects formed in the natal chart.

Sign expression, the common denominator that links eclipse influence to all people, has universal application as observed in eclipse inspired trends and movements. It is personalized in the natal chart. Of the various positive and negative modes of expression associated with a sign, the particular mode that is reinforced in a natal chart manifests more prominently for that individual.

The following generalized interpretations are to be adapted according to initial eclipse influence, duad emphasis and significance in the natal chart.

Solar Eclipse in Aries. A solar eclipse that occupies Aries, the Sun's sign of exaltation, indicates initiative and dynamic action. The Sun's influence in the second decan as its sub-ruler steadies Arian drive; Jupiter's in the third as sub-ruler expands it. On a broad level, international trends reflect the pioneering spirit symbolic of Aries and/or the war-like qualities of Mars, planetary ruler of the sign.

Solar Eclipse in Taurus. In Taurus (ruled by Venus), solar eclipse activity is dependable and stable. Expression is less rigid in the second decan because of Mercury's influence as sub-ruler. In the third decan, Saturn's influence as sub-ruler reinforces reliability. On a universal level, practical considerations and commercialism underlie eclipse activity. Countries become more conscious of their possessions and of their worth as nations.

Solar Eclipse in Gemini. Intellectualism underscores sign expression of a solar eclipse in Gemini (ruled by Mercury). Superficiality may be present if the tendency is activated in the natal chart. Venus' influence in the second decan as sub-ruler lends artistic flair to Gemini expression; Uranus' influence in the third decan as sub-ruler adds a provocative touch. World trends reflect free-flowing communications and an increase in meetings and discussions at national and international levels.

Solar Eclipse in Cancer. A solar eclipse in Cancer (ruled by the Moon) generates sensitivity and feeling. Pluto's influence in the second decan as sub-ruler enhances insight; Neptune's in the third as sub-ruler lends an ethereal quality to Cancerian expression. Domestic priorities become prominent on a universal scale.

Solar Eclipse in Leo. Activity of a solar eclipse in Leo, the Sun's sign of dignity, is expressed with vigor and authority in the theatrical style characteristic of the sign. Expansive Jupiter's influence in the second decan as sub-ruler gives greater scope to Leo expression. Mars' influence in the third decan as sub-ruler hastens action. Leo attributes of leadership and power-seeking manifest in world trends.

Solar Eclipse in Virgo. The discriminating properties of Virgo (ruled by Mercury) are obvious in activity of a solar eclipse placed in the sign. Here, expression is orderly and detailed. In the second decan, Saturn's influence as sub-ruler sponsors greater dedication and reliability. The third decan reflects touches of the earthy charm of Taurean Venus, its sub-ruler. During the effective period of a Virgo solar eclipse, health and job concerns dominate national/international causes.

Solar Eclipse in Libra. Harmony and unity lend a smooth flow to activity of a solar eclipse in Libra (ruled by Venus), the Sun's sign of fall. Expression is less even in the second decan because of unpredictable Uranus' influence as sub-ruler. In the third decan, Mercury's influence as sub-ruler enhances Libran intellectual attributes. General trends assume an essence of justice and fair play during the effective period of the eclipse.

Solar Eclipse in Scorpio. The intensity of Pluto, planetary ruler of Scorpio, manifests in the activity of a solar eclipse that occupies the sign. Expression is forceful, passionate and purposeful. Neptune's influence in the second decan as sub-ruler emphasizes elements of mystery and secrecy. The Moon's influence in the third decan as sub-ruler heightens emotional sensitivity. Spiritual regeneration and/or physical renewal underlie universal causes associated with a solar eclipse in Scorpio.

Solar Eclipse in Sagittarius. Action of a solar eclipse in Sagittarius, ruled by Jupiter, is broad-ranging, philosophical and expansive. The second decan, sub-ruled by Mars, promotes excesses and tendencies to overreach. In the third decan, the influence of its sub-ruler, the Sun, increases stability without reducing vitality of Sagittarian expression. From a broader perspective, organized religion assumes greater significance in world trends. New religious movements frequently begin and/or existing ones flourish under the auspices of a Sagittarius solar eclipse.

Solar Eclipse in Capricorn. Ambition, discipline and pragmatism describe expression of a solar eclipse in Capricorn, ruled by Saturn. As sub-ruler, Venus' influence in the second decan reinforces avaricious tendencies. In the third decan, Mercury's influence as sub-ruler promotes an objective, no-nonsense approach although expression is somewhat less restrictive than in the first two decans because of Mercury's versatility. This solar eclipse promotes traditionalism and conservatism on a broad scale.

Solar Eclipse in Aquarius. In Aquarius, the Sun's sign of detriment, a solar eclipse denotes the progress and change symbolic of the sign and its planetary ruler, Uranus. Expression may be hasty, untimely, even contradictory, but it is innovative as well. As sub-ruler of the second decan, Mercury reinforces the intellectual mode of Aquarian expression. As sub-ruler of the third decan,

Venus warms its impersonal tone. Widespread attention turns to humanitarian concerns during the eclipse period of influence, and social movements flourish.

Solar Eclipse in Pisces. Activity of a solar eclipse in Pisces, ruled by Neptune, is gentle and subdued; it can be haphazard and aimless. Frequently, it is expressed by psychic or spiritual means; usually, it reflects mystical qualitites. The Moon's influence in the second decan as sub-ruler promotes greater emotionalism and sentiment which can be maudlin in nature. In the third decan, sub-ruler Pluto emphasizes the morbid, secretive qualities of sign expression and, in a highly developed chart, reinforces spiritual attributes. During the effective period of a Pisces solar eclipse, spiritual movements attract widespread interest, and religious cults often take shape.

CHAPTER 2

LUNAR ECLIPSES IN THE SIGNS

Lunar eclipses belong to series similar to the Saros solar series and are numbered in like manner. A lunar eclipse always occurs at the node opposite that at which the solar eclipse(s) in the same sequence occur. Thus a 1-S lunar eclipse is followed in about six months by one from the 1-N lunar series in the next sequence which is followed six months later by one from the 2-S series, etc., until the lunar series cycle is completed by a 19-N lunar eclipse that accompanies a 19-S solar eclipse. Both solar and lunar series then begin another cycle with a sequence containing a 1-N solar eclipse and a 1-S lunar eclipse. Dual lunar series which behave similarly to dual solar series interrupt the six-month pattern of lunar eclipse appearance; then a lunar eclipse from the earlier starting lunar series is followed in about a month by one from its replacement series resulting in a triple sequence composed of a lunar eclipse, a solar eclipse and a second lunar eclipse. Study of the table of lunar and solar eclipses in the Appendix can clarify the six-month pattern of eclipse appearances and the anomalies that occur when dual or solar series operate.

The zodiacal positions of appulses that led off lunar series are unknown, so initial eclipse considerations are not part of lunar eclipse sign interpretation. However, other factors merit consideration. Because of the responsive nature of the Moon, a lunar eclipse acts on the inner plane. Its sign expression is more subtle than that of a solar eclipse which occupies the same sign. Too, the zodiacal relationship that exists between signs occupied by a lunar and solar eclipse belonging to the same sequence bears upon interpretation.

In those instances when a lunar eclipse and the solar eclipse it accompanies lie opposite each other in the zodiac, the two signs complement each other. Then, sign qualities manifested on the inner plane (lunar eclipse) support and balance solar eclipse sign expression.

The only other sign combination possible in an eclipse sequence is a quincunx by sign, approaching or departing from the lunar point of view (forward or backward in the zodiac from lunar eclipse to solar eclipse). When a solar and lunar eclipse belonging to the same sequence are placed five signs apart (quincunx by sign), sign expression of the lunar eclipse is somewhat incongruous and often overshadowed by that of the solar eclipse. To utilize lunar expression to the fullest, it is necessary to emphasize lunar modes of sign expression that complement or are similar to solar eclipse sign attributes and to modify those lunar sign traits that clash with solar expression. If the two eclipses in a given sequence share a common duad sub-ruler, that planet provides basis for agreement between their two signs. Other rulership links are pointed out in the following interpretations.

Lunar Eclipse in Aries. Lunar eclipse expression here is stimulating and motivating. In combination with a solar eclipse in Libra (opposite by sign), inner incentive and instinctive responses typical of an Aries lunar eclipse encourage Libran solar eclipse action. Sign polarity between the two eclipses provides balance that is mutually reinforcing, not antagonistic.

When paired with a solar eclipse in Virgo, forming an approaching quincunx by sign, the expression of a lunar eclipse in Aries becomes abrasive. Aries wants action; Virgo strives for perfection. In order to derive the most benefit from this sign combination, the individual must temper the impulsive reaction common to an Aries lunar eclipse to support the meticulous expression natural to a Virgo solar eclipse. This is a matter of degree, for Virgo can use the initiatory qualities of Aries; it is the rashness and impetuosity that must be controlled.

An Aries lunar eclipse can also form a departing quincunx with a solar eclipse in Scorpio. With this configuration, Aries initiative is stifled. The individual must work to release Arian incentive in a manner that induces and promotes purposeful Scorpio expression. Although Mars, dignified in Aries, is generally accepted as co-ruler of Scorpio, it cannot be accepted as an adequate bridge to sign differences since the two signs operate on widely divergent levels of expression.

Lunar Eclipse in Taurus. In the sign of the Moon's exaltation, Taurus, a lunar eclipse expresses emotional constancy and internal serenity. When it is paired with a Scorpio solar eclipse (opposite by sign), the inner strength it generates reinforces the forcefulness and purpose symbolic of Scorpio. Too, this combination carries sensual connotations. Taurus, representing receptive sexuality, and Scorpio, signifying aggressive sexuality, suggest completeness in sexual expression when operating together.

Venus, as planetary ruler of both Taurus and Libra, projects similarities that bridge qualitative sign differences displayed by a Taurus lunar eclipse and a Libra solar eclipse which appear in the same sequence to form an approaching quincunx by sign. Here, Venusian traits as expressed through earthy Taurus produce emotional stability that lends consistency to the harmonious, pleasing qualities associated with Libra.

However, when a Taurus lunar eclipse accompanies a solar eclipse in Sagittarius forming a departing quincunx by sign, one must strive harder to achieve a working rapport between the two. Plodding Taurus is no match for buoyant Sagittarius. To benefit most, one must utilize Taurean inner strengths to undergird Sagittarian expression and relax undue emotional inflexibility.

Lunar Eclipse in Gemini. In Gemini, a lunar eclipse stirs changeable emotions and versatile intellectual instincts. Accompanying a solar eclipse in Sagittarius (opposite by sign), its mercurial inner mode of emotional/mental expression inspires the free-ranging, spirited qualities characteristic of Sagittarius.

In combination with a solar eclipse in Scorpio (approaching quincunx by sign), the versatility of a Gemini lunar eclipse is limited as Scorpio resists change and rejects superficiality. Here, the individual must try to unify the dualistic responsive intellect associated with Gemini toward the single-minded purposes represented by the Scorpio solar eclipse.

Capricorn's insistence upon discipline makes it difficult for the Gemini mode of expression to manifest untrammeled when a Gemini lunar eclipse is part of a sequence containing a Capricorn solar eclipse (departing quincunx by sign). In this instance, the individual must subdue frivolous Gemini tendencies and utilize objective mental qualities as expressed through emotions and instincts aroused by the Gemini lunar eclipse.

Lunar Eclipse in Cancer. In Cancer, the Moon's sign of dignity, a lunar eclipse signifies sensitive emotional responses. When in sequence with a Capricorn solar eclipse (opposite by sign), expression is complementary, for the Cancer lunar eclipse supplies the sensitivity and responsiveness that Capricorn lacks.

Jupiter, exalted in Cancer and dignified in Sagittarius, represents a common bond between a Cancer lunar eclipse and a Sagittarian solar eclipse belonging to the same sequence which form an approaching quincunx by sign. Here, sympathetic facets of lunar expression reinforce idealistic Sagittarian qualities. However, unrestrained lunar emotional responses can promote Sagittarian excesses; therefore, the individual must exercise control and direction.

Unless the individual can raise the intimate mode of Cancerian expression to a more objective level, a Cancer lunar eclipse will be largely ineffective when paired with a solar eclipse in Aquarius (departing quincunx by sign). The Aquarian attitude rejects sentimentality, and subjective Cancer must respond in an impersonal mode if lunar eclipse energy is to be fully utilized.

Lunar Eclipse in Leo. A Leo lunar eclipse fosters emotional vitality and evokes natural creative instincts. In combination with a solar eclipse in Aquarius (opposite by sign), it fires Aquarian expression, lending emotional motivation to Aquarian genius.

When paired with a solar eclipse in Capricorn (approaching quincunx by sign), the ardent and ostentatious qualities associated with a Leo lunar eclipse conflict with Capricornian restraint and discretion. To best utilize lunar eclipse potentials with this configuration, one must accent the leadership and power-seeking attributes of Leo to support Capricornian ambition and status-seeking characteristics.

The combination of a Leo lunar eclipse and a Pisces solar eclipse (departing quincunx by sign) presents a contradictory situation. Pisces does not respond well to fiery Leo's prompting and tends to dampen Leo emotional enthusiasm. However, mutable Pisces can benefit from Leo vigor if the individual utilizes Leo staying power to sustain Piscean activity. Too, Leonine creative instincts reinforce Pisces artistry.

Lunar Eclipse in Virgo. In Virgo, a lunar eclipse stirs inner reticence and discriminating instincts. It operates smoothly with a solar eclipse that occupies Pisces (opposite by sign) - its orderly instinctive mode balancing haphazard Piscean tendencies, its reticent emotional mode agreeing with the gentle, subdued manner symbolic of Pisces expression.

Mercury, dignified in Virgo and exalted in Aquarius, provides some natural affinity between eclipses when a Virgo lunar eclipse is paired with an Aquarius solar eclipse (approaching quincunx by sign). The Aquarian mode of change and innovation balks at Virgo reserve yet finds Virgo adaptability helpful. In proper balance, practical Virgo attributes promote more efficient Aquarian expression.

A Virgo lunar eclipse does not combine readily with a solar eclipse in Aries (departing quincunx by sign). Headstrong Aries tends to ignore the cautionary instincts of Virgo; the brash Arian mode of expression obscures the less confident mode typical of Virgo. This combination works best if the discriminating properties of Virgo can be adapted to Arian eagerness and channeled to particularize Arian endeavor.

Lunar Eclipse in Libra. A lunar eclipse in Libra is unique in that it operates relatively smoothly with solar eclipses in each of the three signs possible for a solar eclipse appearing in the same sequence to occupy. The inner harmony and peaceful instincts it symbolizes offset discordant attributes of Aries without compromising Arian initiative and dynamism when paired with a solar eclipse in that sign (opposite by sign).

A Libra lunar eclipse and a Pisces solar eclipse (approaching quincunx by sign) share an easy rapport since Venus, dignified in Libra and exalted in Pisces, effectively bridges differences that exist between the two signs. Here, lunar and solar expression is mutually compatible with the gentle, obliging emotional reaction of Libra combining well with subtle, responsive Pisces expression.

When a Libra lunar eclipse forms a departing quincunx by sign with a Taurus solar eclipse, attributes of Venus common to both signs span disparities in quality of sign expression. In this configuration, Libran emotional equilibrium supports practical Taurean endeavor. This combination is especially helpful to the artistically inclined, for Libran aesthetic instincts motivate outward expression of Taurean artistic tendencies.

Lunar Eclipse in Scorpio. A lunar eclipse in Scorpio, the Moon's sign of fall, heightens emotional intensity and strengthens inner resolve. Paired with a solar eclipse in Taurus (opposite by sign), it supplements Taurean determination and endurability. Similar to a Taurus lunar/Scorpio solar eclipse combination, this one also has sexual implications.

A Scorpio lunar eclipse paired with an Aries solar eclipse (approaching quincunx by sign) results in an incongruous situation. Symbolically, Aries is off and running before Scorpio gets started. Aries expression is overt; Scorpio's, secretive. Though Mars is generally considered to be dignified in both signs, its natural Arian attributes are incompatible with Scorpio expression, and it does not act as an effective connecting link between the two signs. With this configuration, it is essential that the individual utilize those Scorpio qualities that promote resolve and lend continuity to Arian expression and suppress Scorpio attributes that would smother Arian incentive.

A Scorpio lunar eclipse shares little in common with a Gemini solar eclipse (departing quincunx by sign). However, the natural insight and penetrating instincts it arouses adds to Gemini intellectual expression, promoting shrewdness and intuitive action.

Lunar Eclipse in Sagittarius. A lunar eclipse that appears in Sagittarius gives rise to enthusiastic emotional impulses and optimistic instinctual responses. In combination with a solar eclipse in Gemini (opposite by sign), it promotes free-flowing Gemini expression.

Little common ground exists upon which to bridge sign disparity when a Sagittarian lunar eclipse accompanies a Taurus solar eclipse (approaching quincunx by sign). This eclipse combination operates best if Sagittarian flexibility can be utilized to produce less rigidity in Taurean expression.

A Sagittarian lunar eclipse/Cancer solar eclipse combination (departing quincunx by sign) benefits from dual Jupiterian influence since Jupiter is dignified in Sagittarius and exalted in Cancer. Here, Sagittarian emotional ardor and instinctive versatility augment Cancerian fluidity.

Lunar Eclipse in Capricorn. In Capricorn, the Moon's sign of detriment, a lunar eclipse inhibits emotional responses and stirs ambitious instincts. It balances emotionalism and sentimentality when it accompanies a solar eclipse in Cancer (opposite by sign) without compromising Cancerian sensitivity and receptivity.

A Capricorn lunar eclipse and a Gemini solar eclipse (approaching quincunx by sign) have little affinity for each other. To make the most of this combination, one must modify severe Capricorn traits so that they can be utilized to discipline frivolous Gemini tendencies and channel Gemini expression constructively without restricting the Gemini spirit, for Gemini refuses to operate under emotional restraint.

An eclipse sequence containing a Capricorn lunar eclipse and a Leo solar eclipse (departing quincunx by sign) presents a somewhat stilted situation. Gregarious Leo will not be inhibited by Capricorn's emotional reserve. Nevertheless, the inner ambition spurred by a Capricorn lunar eclipse, when properly directed, reinforces leadership qualities inherent in Leo expression.

Lunar Eclipse in Aquarius. With a lunar eclipse in Aquarius operating, emotional responses lack warmth and predictability, instinctive reactions reflect a bit of the avant-garde and a wry sense of humor manifests on the inner plane. Paired with a solar eclipse in Leo, an Aquarius lunar eclipse motivates originality in Leo expression and acts as leveler for pompous, egocentric Leo attitudes.

The cool, detached, emotional reaction associated with an Aquarius lunar eclipse does not blend well with the sensitive, responsive nature of a Cancer solar eclipse when the two appear in the same sequence (approaching quincunx by sign). With this combination, it is most helpful to draw upon Aquarian humanitarian instincts in support of Cancerian sympathies, to accent innovative Aquarian qualities and discourage radical characteristics.

Mercury, exalted in Aquarius and dignified in Virgo, bridges some sign differences when a lunar eclipse in Aquarius accompanies a solar eclipse in Virgo (departing quincunx by sign). Here, Aquarian intellectual emotionalism supports analytical attributes and discriminating properties of Virgo.

Lunar Eclipse in Pisces. Emotional apathy, psychic sensitivity and spiritualistic instincts are aroused by a lunar eclipse in Pisces. Paired with a solar eclipse in Virgo (opposite by sign), it enhances intuitive faculties that augment Virgo's drive for detail and accuracy.

When a Pisces lunar eclipse accompanies a Leo solar eclipse (approaching quincunx by sign), spirited Leo expression overwhelms that of subdued Pisces. Artistic/creative qualities intrinsic to both signs, though expressed differently, represent common elements upon which one can draw to best utilize sign potentials of both eclipses.

Venus, exalted in Pisces and dignified in Libra, generates a compatible rapport between the two eclipses when a Pisces lunar eclipse appears in the same sequence as a Libra solar eclipse forming a departing quincunx by sign. In this configuration, gentle, sensitive Piscean emotional responses reinforce Libran potentials for balance and harmony.

CHAPTER 3

SOLAR ECLIPSES IN THE HOUSES

Although the transiting Moon and transiting Sun are astrologically unified by conjunction during a solar eclipse, concurrent oppositions between Earth and the luminaries more aptly describe the motivating effect solar eclipses have in human behavior. For the duration of its effective period, a solar eclipse brings into prominent focus affairs of the house it occupies. The individual grows aware of needs associated with these affairs. He or she seeks to fulfill those needs through some form of ego satisfaction or self-development, for solar eclipse energies are directly associated with the ego, the self. Accordingly, self-expression is directed into affairs of the occupied house enabling the individual to grow, to expand self-awareness as this awareness relates to affairs of the house.

Response to eclipse stimuli is both psychological and physical; psychological response motivates outward behavior. Each individual reacts in a unique manner dictated by natal potentials and prior developmental progress to develop the selfhood through avenues influenced by a solar eclipse. Eclipse-inspired growth takes place on both spiritual and mundane planes.

The affairs of a house are many-sided, and a solar eclipse can activate any or all facets. Basic house meanings given here should be broadened to include related potentials reflected in a particular chart of interest.

The following interpretations embrace a single house focus; further in this chapter, combined house foci created by polar sets of solar eclipses are described and interpreted.

Solar Eclipse in the Natal First House. A solar eclipse that occupies the first house of a natal chart plays a key role in personal development. Self-recognition is essential to self-esteem and to growth. Acknowledgement of weaknesses is as important to development as is recognition of strengths. Some people suffer identity crises or entertain self-doubts as part of the growth process. The period of eclipse influence is one in which the individual who realizes his or her personal potentials can develop and utilize them more fully. Self-knowledge, self-confidence and self-enrichment lead to character building and expansion of personal horizons for those who respond positively to solar eclipse energies. A negative reaction blocks growth potentials and gives rise to smugness and complacency. Many of these people, satisfied with themselves as they are, fail to recognize what they can become. Others who respond negatively overemphasize character flaws and disregard developmental potentials of personal assets.

Solar Eclipse in the Natal Second House. The effective period of a second house solar eclipse marks a time when financial perspectives come into focus. The individual takes pride in his/her personal possessions and financial assets. Ego drives prompt one to seek financial and material status. In response, one person may attempt to increase income (and thereby derive ego satisfaction) by expanding resources; another may try to amass assets through savings or other means; another may acquire huge debts in order to obtain material objects that build the ego; yet still another whose self-pride hinges on displays of generosity may compromise financial well-being by making unaffordable donations and buying extravagant presents. Thus the eclipse period can be a contradictory one whose potentials range from comparative prosperity to economic disaster. However, growth has to do with more than financial activity; the main point of focus deals with the development of material values and stewardship attitudes that foster inner growth as well as material security. Sexual aspects of a second house solar eclipse are discussed further in this chapter under *Second/eighth - Eighth/second House Polar Sets.*

Solar Eclipse in the Natal Third House. Activity of a third house solar eclipse sparks intellectual and communicative needs. The individual derives self-satisfaction through learning and teaching - not teaching in the professional sense unless the person is a teacher, but teaching by outwardly expressing ideas and knowledge in conversation or the written word.

Natal potentials described by the third house and related factors determine whether one turns to reading, study, or intellectual associates and activities to further mental development. Regardless of intellectual avenues the individual chooses to pursue, one grows more mentally aware of the environment in which he or she lives and gains practical knowledge through day-to-day contacts and experiences.

Solar Eclipse in the Natal Fourth House. For most people, a solar eclipse that occupies the fourth house lends incentive to establish the sort of home life that confers personal status and security. Individual response may be directed toward improving physical characteristics of living quarters or toward enhancing family relationships or both. Frequently a residential move occurs during the period of eclipse influence.

Interests to do with parents or members of the household are important factors in events of the period. The period reflects change and adjustment through which the individual strives for a more ego satisfying and enriching family lifestyle.

Solar Eclipse in the Natal Fifth House. The Sun is at home in the fifth house, and here a solar eclipse stirs the need to express oneself creatively and affectionately in accordance with natal potentials. Outer manifestations of creativity and love inspire spiritual development since the fifth house and its planetary ruler, the Sun, represent the soul and life essence.

The individual emphasizes interests and relationships that afford enjoyment and create happy feelings as a means of ego enhancement. A parent often finds that during the eclipse period the relationship with offspring fosters inner growth and ego satisfaction. It is important to positive self-development that fifth house relationships reflect an equal balance of give and take, that one does not exploit them for selfish reasons, for such action blocks developmental potentials.

Solar Eclipse in the Natal Sixth House. A person becomes acutely aware of the need to serve during the effective period of a sixth house solar eclipse. The state of health, employment conditions and job relationships are dominating factors in the developmental process since imperfections in these spheres hinder one's capacity to serve. A positive response to eclipse activity results in better general health and the adoption of good hygienic and nutritional practices, for one finds ego satisfaction in a healthy body. The period also favors action to improve work-related health hazards such as inadequate safety procedures and polluted job environment. One who responds negatively either ignores opportunities to better job and health conditions or becomes preoccupied with them. If a tendency toward hypochondria exists in the natal chart, it often manifests under the influence of a sixth house solar eclipse.

Solar Eclipse in the Natal Seventh House. In the seventh house, a solar eclipse brings into focus needs for human interaction on a one to one basis and with the public in general. A sense of incompleteness prompts the individual to seek a counterpart with whom personal needs are mutually satisfied. In order to enhance self-esteem, one endeavors to form meaningful alliances such as marital or business partnerships, to strengthen existing seventh house relationships that satisfy and to dissolve those that are unfulfilling. Unity and balance are important to development. Ego satisfaction depends as much upon the capacity to fulfill another person's needs as it does upon deriving personal satisfaction from a relationship.

Solar Eclipse in the Natal Eighth House. A solar eclipse in the eighth house acts on material, physical and/or inner planes. Stimulation of the material plane activates the inheritance potential contained in the natal chart and financial interests shared with the marriage partner or business associates. Activation of the physical plane arouses aggressive sexual urges. Inner plane response emphasizes spiritual evolution and psychic development. Direction of an individual's motivation depends upon ego related needs dominant at the time of the eclipse and the growth level attained previously.

Solar Eclipse in the Natal Ninth House. A ninth house solar eclipse heralds a period dedicated primarily to development of abstract throught. One tends to question moral standards, religious practices and theoretical issues in the attempt to develop a personal philosophy and ethical guidelines that give structure to his or her beliefs. During that period of eclipse influence, higher education, travel experiences and other ninth house affairs contribute to the individual's search for truth and wisdom.

Solar Eclipse in the Natal Tenth House. Career advancement and status represent the main theme behind activity inspired by a solar eclipse that occupies the tenth house. One becomes concerned with worldly position and public recognition and usually experiences an inner sense of urgency that prompts concentrated endeavors toward furthering these objectives. In order to derive ego satisfaction, the individual strives for concrete evidence (promotion, raise, public acknowledgement, etc.) that his or her worldy efforts are worthy of merit and productive of success.

Solar Eclipse in the Natal Eleventh House. A solar eclipse that occupies the eleventh house arouses needs associated with one's role as a member of society and the human race. Group interests gain priority over those which are strictly self-oriented. It is through eleventh house relationships and experiences that one's humanitarian attitudes develop. Since self-enhancement is derived principally through love in terms of friendship and genuine human concern during the effective period of an eleventh house solar eclipse, development follows these lines.

Solar Eclipse in the Natal Twelfth House. The effective period of a twelfth house solar eclipse is devoted primarily to phsychological development and spiritual growth. Outer manifestations of eclipse activity have comparable impact upon the inner person. One grows increasingly aware of the interdependency that exists between the physical and spiritual natures. Psychological phobias and suppressed desires described in the natal chart can manifest during the period as can deceitful and fraudulent tendencies. The hidden side of one's nature becomes more apparent or active for better or for worse. In the case of the latter, growth depends upon proper corrective action.

Polar Sets of Solar Eclipses

As eclipses annually regress through the zodiac, solar eclipses belonging to several consecutive sequences frequently alternate between the same two opposite houses of a horoscope producing a continued polar focus. The developmental cycle that covers the period during which two opposite houses are continually activated by a polar set is part of a cyclic growth pattern. Learning experiences encountered during a particular developmental cycle provide the basis for further, more advanced experiences and greater growth when future polar sets activate the same pair of opposite houses.

A polar set unites activity of the two houses involved providing a combined focus in which development in one area (house) supports growth in the other. One's reaction to the stimulus of a polar set and attendant development during a cycle period depends upon natal potentials, maturity and prior growth patterns. An infant does not respond to eclipse stimuli in the same manner as an adult does, but age is no barrier to reaction. Nor does a person react to a second or third similar polar set in the same way as to the first. Developmental progress achieved during one polar set cycle hinges in part upon growth achieved in prior similar cycles.

In the following polar set interpretations, the house listed first is the one activated initially by the first solar eclipse belonging to that polar set. For example, a second/eighth house polar set is one in which the first solar eclipse of a series to activate either house during that cycle occupies the second house; an eighth/second house polar set is initiated by an eighth house solar eclipse. Although in either case interpretation is essentially the same, interpretational orientation varies with the leading eclipse as noted in the interpretations.

The polar set interpretations, intended as guidelines which cover only a few facets of house focus, are to be read in conjunction with meanings given in the forepart of this chapter for solar eclipses in the houses of interest, expanded accordingly and adapted to the individual's frame of reference in terms of age, experience and circumstances at the time the developmental cycle takes place.

First/seventh - Seventh/first House Polar Sets. Here, developmental focus combines personal growth needs with relationship needs. With a first/seventh house focus, identity-seeking and personal expression, getting to know one's self and become at ease with one's self, enable one to reach out into society and establish fulfilling relationships. With a seventh/first house focus, seventh house relationships foster greater self-awareness and confidence enabling one to overcome personal failings and negative attitudes. With either orientation, needs described by the two houses are mutually supportive.

Second/eighth - Eighth/second House Polar Sets. Personal material needs and sharing needs combine to lend emphasis to financial development that extends beyond the personal realm of the second house into the broader sphere of interest described by the eighth house when a polar set of solar eclipses stimulates the two houses. Values and stewardship as identified by the second house are part of development as are spiritual and occult interests (eighth house). One becomes aware of the relationship between the near future (second house) and the distant future - death and life after death (eighth house). Polar set activation of these two houses links receptive sexual needs (second house) with aggressive sexual needs (eighth house); sexual responses are more common to an eighth/second house polar set than to a second/eighth house set.

Third/ninth - Ninth/third House Polar Sets. These polar sets combine concrete mental needs with higher intellectual needs. Developmental focus is directed toward learning, communicating, expanding intellectually and gaining wisdom. With a third/ninth house orientation, one tends to reach out into broad areas of experiential learning through travel or study as he or she learns to relate to his/her environment. Third house experiences provide a foundation for ninth house experiences through which one develops a personal philosophy. With a ninth/third house orientation, philosophical, ethical and/or religious beliefs more prominently color thinking and mental expression.

Fourth/tenth - Tenth/fourth House Polar Sets. Here, security needs, the need to nurture and be nurtured, combine with status and power-seeking needs. The dual influence can be difficult to handle, for balance between family and worldy needs is imperative to progress. The home-oriented or insecure person tends to pour excessive time and energy into creating the kind of home life that gives ego satisfaction, especially if the leading solar eclipse of the polar set falls in the fourth house of the natal horoscope. The career-minded person often neglects family interests in the effort to achieve public distinction. The ideal situation is one in which family and worldly interests are mutually reinforcing.

Fifth/eleventh - Eleventh/fifth House Polar Sets. These polar sets create a solar eclipse focus that balances the need to give love with the need to receive love. With a fifth/eleventh house orientation, personal affectional needs prompt one to reach out into society. As love extends from the personal sphere into societal levels, expression of concern and caring for the human condition manifests. With an eleventh/fifth house orientation, one's sense of universal love lends to higher expression of romantic love. These polar sets bring out one's creative urges (creation of objets d'art, children, etc.) and contribute to development of creative self-expression.

Sixth/twelfth - Twelfth/sixth house Polar Sets. The combined focus of these polar sets deals with the need to serve (sixth house) as described by karmic needs (twelfth house) and links health needs to spiritual well-being. Regardless of orientation, these polar sets produce awareness of needs associated with life - sleep, nutrition, responsibility, job demands - and needs associated with the inner self - spiritual enlightenment, hidden motives, secret anxieties and karmic obligations. They define a period during which one delves into the inner self and expresses spiritual truths in a concrete way in the real world.

Case studies that reflect how different people in various age groups react to polar set stimuli and the growth patterns which emerge during particular developmental cycles are discussed in *Eclipses: Astrological Guideposts*, Chapter 3.

CHAPTER 4

LUNAR ECLIPSES IN THE HOUSES

Earthlings tend to be more emotionally expressive during a Full Moon when Earth and the transiting Moon move into conjunction, both planets opposing the transiting Sun. A lunar eclipse, occurring as it does during a Full Moon and operating on a subjective level, emphasizes this emotional reaction. Unlike a solar eclipse which arouses ego related needs, a lunar eclipse stirs inner needs that are essentially emotional, instinctive and psychic. One's response to eclipse sequence stimulation is twofold as he or she tries to satisfy needs of the self-nature which seek ego satisfaction (solar eclipse) and those of the inner nature which seek emotional fulfillment (lunar eclipses).

The house position of a lunar eclipse indicates avenues which, if approached positively, can be utilized to support activity of the solar eclipse(s) belonging to the same sequence. The extent of development achieved during an eclipse period depends in part upon emotional attitudes described by the lunar eclipse and the capacity to derive inner satisfaction through lunar house activities.

Interpretational variations based upon the order of eclipse appearance in a given sequence place a fine distinction between reactive and active modes of lunar expression, although in either case lunar response is subjective. A lunar eclipse that leads a sequence elicits preparatory responses; one's reaction to lunar house conditions and situations can produce positive changes necessary so that lunar energies fully support activity of the forthcoming solar eclipse. A lunar eclipse that appears later in a sequence than a solar eclipse it accompanies points to action in the lunar house that reinforces development in the solar house. This situation suggests greater emotional initiative than that produced by a leading lunar eclipse.

The relationship between the houses of a horoscope occupied by lunar and solar members of an eclipse sequence lends particular nuances to interpretation. A lunar and solar pair of eclipses that occupy opposite houses (not necessarily opposite signs) focuses on complementary emotional (lunar eclipse) and egocentric needs (solar eclipse) according to hemisphere emphasis, balancing personal needs (northern hemisphere) with dispersive (southern hemisphere) and independent needs (eastern hemisphere) with dependent (western hemisphere). An angle of distress formed by an eclipse pair (lunar and solar eclipses placed five houses apart in the horoscope), regardless of sign positions, indicates a disproportionate situation that requires directed effort to produce and maintain equilibrium. This configuration describes inner frustrations and negative attitudes which, if uncorrected, hinder developmental progress in the solar house as well as in lunar affairs.

In those instances when a single lunar eclipse accompanies two solar eclipses in one sequence, differing relationships that exist between each solar eclipse and the lunar eclipse shade interpretation accordingly. When two lunar eclipses accompany one solar eclipse in a single sequence, each lunar eclipse is interpreted according to its place in the sequence and its relationship to the solar eclipse.

Lunar Eclipse in the Natal First House. One's instinctive response to a first house lunar eclipse depends upon emotional attitudes portrayed in the natal chart. The individual senses an emotional emptiness that motivates changes in the personal sphere to fill the inner void. One usually tries to develop a self-image that gives inner satisfaction.

A first house lunar eclipse/seventh house solar eclipse combination balances personal emotional needs with self-enhancing relationship needs. Mutually supportive interaction between the two houses promotes personal satisfaction and the capacity to establish meaningful relationships.

A first house lunar eclipse/sixth house solar eclipse pair suggests that emotional problems and/or faulty personal attitudes revealed by the lunar eclipse are the source of health setbacks, inharmonious job relationships or other sixth house difficulties that interfere with complete solar eclipse development.

A first house lunar eclipse/eighth house solar eclipse configuration points to the necessity of overcoming negative instincts and fatalistic attitudes described by the lunar eclipse. It calls for development of positive personal traits that can be productive of advancement in eighth house affairs.

Lunar Eclipse in the Natal Second House. With a lunar eclipse activating the second house, one tends to be somewhat emotionally dependent upon financial security. Financial fluctuations that lend to emotional uneasiness usually occur during the period of eclipse influence. In order to preserve emotional well-being, many people respond by trying to stabilize financial interests; others, at a loss as to how to handle economic changes, often drain themselves emotionally and financially.

A second house lunar eclipse/eighth house solar eclipse pair promotes balanced financial perspectives and a growing sense of the relationship between material and spiritual values.

The angle of distress formed between a second house lunar eclipse and a seventh house solar eclipse directs attention to emotional/financial considerations that color seventh house interaction. People inclined to marry for money often do so under the influence of this eclipse configuration.

A second house lunar eclipse/ninth house solar eclipse combination suggests that financial issues underlie philosophical development during the period of eclipse activity. Afflictions identify contradictions that exist between materialistic attitudes and ethical practices or religious beliefs.

Lunar Eclipse in the Natal Third House. A lunar eclipse in the third house lends emotional and psychic touches to mental perceptions; feelings play a larger role in the reasoning process. One grows more intuitive and imaginative during the period of eclipse influence and seeks inner satisfaction from mental accomplishments.

A third house lunar eclipse/ninth house solar eclipse pair produces an atmosphere conducive to higher intellectual development, for here basic mental skills support intellectual growth on a broad scale.

A third house lunar eclipse/eighth house solar eclipse combination points out the need to adjust negative mental/emotional attitudes that inhibit development of eighth house affairs. One must develop more positive and objective approaches to third and eighth house matters.

A third house lunar eclipse/tenth house solar eclipse arrangement implies that overly emotional decisions and failure to develop natal mental potentials restrict worldly progress. In this instance, one must attempt to utilize common sense and expand mental skills to support tenth house ambitions.

Lunar Eclipse in the Natal Fourth House. In the fourth house, the Moon's domain, a lunar eclipse evokes domestic/family instincts. Since inner security and emotional fulfillment depend upon family relationships and domestic stability, one tries to create the type of home atmosphere and family life in which he or she feels emotionally secure.

When paired with a tenth house solar eclipse, a fourth house lunar eclipse lends emotional support to worldly ambitions. One's inner sense of purpose backs up and reinforces ambitious drives expressed in tenth house affairs.

A fourth house lunar eclipse/ninth house solar eclipse combination indicates that home and family life influences one's capacity to reach out intellectually through higher education or travel and that lack of an emotionally supportive domestic atmosphere can hinder intellectual/philosophical growth.

A fourth house lunar eclipse/eleventh house solar eclipse pair denotes family-based emotional insecurities and attitudes developed during early childhood as playing major roles in adult humanitarian concepts and, perhaps, as blocks to one's capacity to form productive eleventh house relationships.

Lunar Eclipse in the Natal Fifth House. A lunar eclipse in the fifth house accents emotional/affectional needs associated with children, romance, pleasure and creative expression. One instinctively seeks inner satisfaction through fifth house relationships, entertaining activities and the hobbies he or she enjoys.

Feelings of emotional well-being derived from fifth house interests and relationships support development of eleventh house potentials when a solar eclipse in that house is paired with a lunar eclipse in the fifth.

A fifth house lunar eclipse/tenth house solar eclipse combination indicates lack of perspective between pleasurable interests and worldly affairs; usually, the individual becomes overly occupied with career advancement and other tenth house matters to the exclusion of fifth house activities unless a conscientious effort is made to balance emotional and ego-related needs. In this instance, business and pleasure do mix well, and it is up to the individual to adjust attention accordingly.

A fifth house lunar eclipse/twelfth house solar eclipse pair produces a contrary situation. In order that the growth potential be reached, one must adjust fifth house affairs so that they do not conflict with the spiritual potential of the twelfth house and yet still produce inner satisfaction. With this configuration, it is most productive to emphasize spiritual and creative aspects of the fifth house rather than the mundane.

Lunar Eclipse in the Natal Sixth House. A lunar eclipse in the sixth house stresses the importance of emotional well-being to one's state of health and the job atmosphere. One usually tries to form relationships in the work sphere with persons in whose company he or she feels emotionally secure and comfortable.

A sixth house lunar eclipse/twelfth house solar eclipse arrangement balances the physical and the spiritual; sixth house interests reinforce twelfth house development.

A sixth house lunar eclipse/eleventh house solar eclipse combination suggests that health and work-related frustrations compromise one's capacity to reach out in humanitarian love. If deficiencies in the sixth house go unchanged and helpful sixth house avenues remain unrecognized, selfish motivations emerge as overriding factors in eleventh house development.

A sixth house lunar eclipse/first house solar eclipse pair emphasizes the influence that one's emotional attitudes toward work, service and health have upon personal growth. Without proper balance between affairs of the two houses, needs of the self are overemphasized. Lunar eclipse afflictions describe negative job attitudes and inadequate health/hygiene habits that detract from physical well-being and hinder character development.

Lunar Eclipse in the Natal Seventh House. With a lunar eclipse in the seventh house, emotional drives motivate one to form and sustain emotionally fulfilling seventh house relationships. During the period of eclipse influence, some people drift out of emotionally empty relationships while others, more forceful, sever ties abruptly if separative potentials are confirmed in the horoscope.

Paired with a first house solar eclipse, a seventh house lunar eclipse fosters emotionally secure relationships that encourage mature personal development described by the solar eclipse.

A seventh house lunar eclipse/twelfth house solar eclipse combination shows that one needs to reach out to others on an emotional level in order to fully develop spiritual potentials of the twelfth house.

A seventh house lunar eclipse/second house solar eclipse pair stresses one's need for emotionally satisfying social interaction and partnerships that support financial growth and evolving material attitudes.

Lunar Eclipse in the Natal Eighth House. A lunar eclipse in the eighth house, an occult house, seldom accents only materialistic aspects of the house. Usually, it also stirs psychic needs and instincts to do with afterlife. Careful study of the natal potentials of the eighth house in relation to the emphasis shown by the solar eclipse(s) in the sequence can shed light on the main direction of an individual's response.

With an eighth house lunar eclipse/second house solar eclipse arrangement, one's sensitivity to eighth house affairs and the steps taken to achieve inner fulfillment balances personal financial drives associated with the second house. Here, satisfying inner values can promote higher material values.

An eighth house lunar eclipse/first house solar eclipse pair calls attention to eighth house avenues that can support personal development (first house) and those which do not. It is important to personal growth that the individual correct eighth house attitudes that hinder character development or promote selfishness.

An eighth house lunar eclipse/third house solar eclipse combination proves most fruitful if the individual emphasizes the psychic aspects of the eighth house to give instinctive and intuitive support to development of the intellect as described by solar eclipse potentials.

Lunar Eclipse in the Natal Ninth House. When a lunar eclipse activates the ninth house, one tends to turn toward religious affiliations and cultural interests for emotional fulfillment. Travel becomes more appealing, and those who are naturally restless often experience a sense of overwhelming wanderlust.

The activity of a ninth house lunar eclipse that is paired with a third house solar eclipse usually follows intellect-expanding lines that reinforce third house mental development.

With a ninth house lunar eclipse/second house solar eclipse combination, the higher intellect and other ninth house affairs promote financial interests if any blocks shown by the lunar eclipse are removed. Here, faulty ethical/moral attitudes can inhibit second house progress.

A ninth house lunar eclipse/fourth house solar eclipse configuration merges ethical and cultural values with family interests; cultural and/or religious biases, if revealed in the horoscope, represent barriers to the evolution of an ego-satisfying home life and secure family relationships.

Lunar Eclipse in the Natal Tenth House. One seeks career endeavors that are emotionally satisfying when a lunar eclipse occupies the tenth house and instinctively turns to avenues and associated relationships that provide inner satisfaction. One derives a sense of inner fulfillment in his or her worldly accomplishments that differs from the ego satisfaction and self-pride sought in public recognition when a solar eclipse occupies the tenth house.

It is this inner satisfaction and sense of emotional well-being derived from worldly interests that contributes to progress of family affairs when a tenth house lunar eclipse is paired with a fourth house solar eclipse.

In combination with a third house solar eclipse, a tenth house lunar eclipse directs attention to fruitful career avenues and identifies futile or inadequate lines of endeavor. In order that third house development (solar eclipse) reach full potential and related experiences be put to practical use, it is important that one pursue positive tenth house directions.

A tenth house lunar eclipse/fifth house solar eclipse configuration emphasizes pleasure-seeking and other fifth house matters over worldly ambitions and brings out hedonistic tendencies if such exist in the natal chart. It is easier for the career-minded person to establish suitable balance between the two houses than it is for the person who has little worldly ambition. In any case, it is important that the individual respond to needs of both houses so that tenth house activity supports fifth house progress along productive lines.

Lunar Eclipse in the Natal Eleventh House. A lunar eclipse in the eleventh house denotes a period during which one derives emotional satisfaction through participation in group activities and humanitarian causes. This placement brings out altruistic instincts and creates inner awareness of the need to play an unselfish role in the society to which one belongs.

The inner security one gains through eleventh house activities and relationships reinforces the capacity to sustain romantic relationships, to express oneself creatively and to enjoy life according to the promise of the fifth house when an eleventh house lunar eclipse accompanies a fifth house solar eclipse.

An eleventh house lunar eclipse/fourth house solar eclipse combination indicates that, in order to effectively utilize interests of both houses, it is helpful to host group meetings and entertain friends in the home. With this configuration, it is important that eleventh house attitudes and activities be modified to accommodate developmental needs of the fourth house.

An eleventh house lunar eclipse that appears in the same sequence as a sixth house solar eclipse suggests that one broaden eleventh house interests to include organizations that complement the need to serve and those devoted to health and other sixth house affairs. It also points to emotional biases reflected in the eleventh house which, if not eliminated, hinder development in both houses.

Lunar Eclipse in the Natal Twelfth House. In the twelfth house, a lunar eclipse rouses the subconscious and stirs psychic and spiritual tendencies. One instinctively reaches out to the intangible realm for emotional support and usually grows more receptive to psychic/spiritual influences.

Paired with a sixth house solar eclipse, a twelfth house lunar eclipse generates substantial psychological support to sixth house development. It also brings out natural instincts that encourage good health care practices.

In sequence with a fifth house solar eclipse, a twelfth house lunar eclipse points to hidden inhibitions or psychological blocks that interfere with fifth house expression. It calls for close scrutiny of emotional attitudes described in the twelfth house that influence one's relationship with offspring, one's approach to romance, one's creative self-expression and other fifth house matters.

A twelfth house lunar eclipse, when combined with a seventh house solar eclipse, suggests that the individual examine unsatisfactory seventh house relationships from a karmic standpoint as described by the twelfth house and its interrelationship with the seventh. Once relationship problems are identified, one can determine the proper approach to correct them and improve related situations.

CHAPTER 5

SOLAR ECLIPSE ASPECTS

Although the main focus of solar eclipse activity centers in the natal house the eclipse occupies, its energies are distributed elsewhere in the chart via the planets it aspects. Hard aspects call attention to obstacles, conflicts or tensions (according to the nature of the aspect) with which one must deal in order that the full potential of eclipse activity be utilized. They also describe the nature of potential experiences and events which can manifest during the effective period of eclipse influence. Refer to "Manifestation of Eclipse Related Events" in Chapter 7. Easy aspects point out those avenues, situations and relationships through which the eclipse potential can be developed relatively unimpeded, areas that promote growth.

Major zodiacal eclipse aspects are more influential in a horoscope than minor ones. The quincunx, strongest of the minor aspects, ranks close to major aspects in strength. Other hard minor aspects carry almost as much emphasis as the quincunx. Minor easy aspects, parallels, contraparallels and out of sign aspects (major and minor) carry least weight in a horoscope; in combination with other aspects, they play an amplifying or modifying role.

The orb for major zodiacal eclipse aspects is limited to 5 degrees, to 2 degrees for minor aspects and to 1 degree for parallels and contraparallels. Exact aspects (1 degree orb) are considered stronger than those with wider orbs. Exact major hard zodiacal aspects and quincunxes are most commonly associated with eclipse related events and experiences that have lasting impact upon the individual.

When interpreting eclipse aspects, one must adapt the meanings given to include sign significance, house emphasis and the influence of other aspects formed by the eclipse and the aspected planet.

TRANSITING SOLAR ECLIPSE ASPECTS TO NATAL SUN

Solar eclipse aspects to the natal Sun bring natal potentials of the Sun into sharp focus. One becomes keenly aware of the need to set his or her own course, to be what he or she wants to be. Because the capacity to master areas activated by these aspects is a matter of self-pride, the individual is drawn toward those areas even if they are afflicted. The period of eclipse influence is vital to self-development.

Transiting Solar Eclipse Conjunct Natal Sun. Situations and experiences associated with this aspect promote self-interest in the affairs activated. The individual places great importance upon the capacity to assume the leading role in managing and directing these affairs. Increased vitality marks the period of eclipse influence unless the conjunction is severely afflicted; then the individual must pace energies in order not to severely drain natural vitality. An exact conjunction creates the potential for a major event of the type that proves to be a milestone in life.

Transiting Solar Eclipse Sextile Natal Sun. This sextile promises opportunities that enable one to fully develop the self through the affairs energized in accordance with prevailing circumstances and prior progress. It creates an atmosphere that enhances self-confidence and optimism. The individual is inspired to attempt high accomplishments, to exercise authority and to express the creative self.

Transiting Solar Eclipse Square Natal Sun. This square points to ego-related obstacles that stand in the way of self-development. Over-confidence and conceit can lead the individual to overreach or expect too much from himself/herself in related affairs. Self-will is much in evidence here and must be channeled constructively if activated areas are to progress fully. Honest self-appraisal is important to positive growth. Possible setbacks associated with this aspect are of the sort that help rid one of ego-related barriers and lead to a more objective self-opinion.

Transiting Solar Eclipse Trine Natal Sun. This aspect generates conditions conducive to self-development during the period in which the eclipse remains active. Affairs energized by the solar eclipse benefit from circumstances surrounding those ruled and influenced by the natal Sun and vice versa. Solar eclipse energies help one overcome problems inherent in natal Sun afflictions. Leadership potentials and self-drives described by the natal Sun respond to developmental avenues suggested by solar eclipse activity.

Transiting Solar Eclipse Quincunx Natal Sun. Under the influence of this aspect one grows conscious of esoteric implications in relationships with the father, offspring and, in a woman's chart, the husband. One's reaction depends largely upon the state of the ego and prior development. However, this quincunx alerts one to the importance of making adjustments in these relationships as part of karmic progress. Events that manifest as a result of activation of this aspect contain lessons that may or may not be recognized by the individual as such at the time, but these lessons always have impact upon one's karma.

Transiting Solar Eclipse Opposite Natal Sun. With this aspect, ego needs stirred by the eclipse oppose basic natal ego needs, and it is only by coordinating apparently conflicting needs to establish a compatible balance that one can realize full developmental potentials of the eclipse period. This opposition points out character flaws and lacks that, when corrected, harmonize creative self-expression and ego drives. Events that correspond to this opposition represent turning points that offer new directions.

TRANSITING SOLAR ECLIPSE ASPECTS TO NATAL MOON

Solar eclipse aspects to the natal Moon stimulate the emotions and elicit emotional responses in keeping with natal potentials. They link emotional growth to the self-developmental potential described by the solar eclipse. Negative reactions to events and experiences stemming from affairs associated with hard eclipse aspects hamper developmental progress and can create serious emotional blocks.

Transiting Solar Eclipse Conjunct Natal Moon. This aspect brings emotional and instinctive drives described by the natal Moon into focus. Solar eclipse activity reflects sensitivity and feeling in accordance with the natal potential for emotional expression. This conjunction also brings into play emotional problems and inner frustrations shown by afflictions to the natal Moon. Its influence extends into affairs ruled by and aspected by the natal Moon. Events associated with this aspect have emotional impact upon the individual, and in the case of an exact conjunction, the effect can be traumatic, especially if the conjunction is severely afflicted.

Transiting Solar Eclipse Sextile Natal Moon. This sextile has a calming effect upon the individual as solar eclipse energies harmonize with feelings. It points out opportune areas that extend from the house occupied by the solar eclipse to those occupied, ruled and aspected by the natal Moon, areas in which solar eclipse energy can be directed productively toward positive growth experiences. One usually feels good about associated activities and interests and instinctively pursues these affairs. This sextile also creates an atmosphere helpful to overcoming emotional blocks shown by afflictions to the natal Moon, thus enabling one to constructively channel energies generated by the afflictions.

Transiting Solar Eclipse Square Natal Moon. The period during which this square is in effect (the duration of solar eclipse influence) can be an emotionally frustrating one, especially if the natal Moon is afflicted, for solar eclipse activity is directed into natal lunar potentials. With a wide square, the effect may be no more than the manifestation of a tendency to drag one's feet rather than actively pursue affairs influenced by the aspect. An exact square usually heralds a major event that can be emotionally shattering. If the natal Moon is well aspected, this square identifies momentary emotional attitudes that arise during the eclipse period, attitudes which can inhibit solar eclipse progress if allowed to develop along negative lines.

Transiting Solar Eclipse Trine Natal Moon. This trine facilitates solar eclipse action and indicates circumstances, avenues and associations that contribute to positive learning experiences. It does not change the nature of events described by concurrent hard solar eclipse aspects, but it does help enable one to utilize those experiences constructively. It lends to the capacity to deal with adversities and to grow stronger because of, or perhaps in spite of, them.

Transiting Solar Eclipse Quincunx Natal Moon. This aspect reveals karmic responsibilities involving one's family, especially the mother, and/or, in a man's chart, the wife. Relevant situations that arise during the period of eclipse influence should be studied for karmic implications. People who come into one's life at the time often share family karma if comparison of the natal charts verifies the potential. Events and experiences associated with this quincunx deal with one's karmic progress in relation to family karma.

Transiting Solar Eclipse Opposite Natal Moon. This opposition creates much emotional tension. Although attendant emotional conflicts can make it difficult to utilize solar eclipse energy productively, they create awareness of innate emotional weaknesses and, if the individual responds positively, enable him or her to overcome inborn emotional handicaps. Events associated with an exact opposition can leave lasting emotional scars.

TRANSITING SOLAR ECLIPSE ASPECTS TO NATAL MERCURY

A solar eclipse aspect to natal Mercury arouses mental energies and motivates the individual to utilize intellectual and communicative skills. One usually responds in a manner designed to elicit admiration from the people associated with affairs influenced by the aspect. One's pride in mental prowess is the motivating factor behind efforts to advance these interests.

Transiting Solar Eclipse Conjunct Natal Mercury. This conjunction energizes natural mental aptitudes. The individual derives much ego satisfaction through developing and displaying intellectual abilities. The urge to express thoughts through speech and/or writing and to exercise personal judgment in affairs influenced by this aspect grows more pronounced during the eclipse effective period in accordance with the sign and house position of the conjunction. Correct reasoning and constructive planning are essential to development promised by solar eclipse activity. Events associated with this conjunction produce intellectual impressions that have much to do with acquiring broader mental concepts. Eclipse related experiences may involve a brother or sister.

Transiting Solar Eclipse Sextile Natal Mercury. Affairs influenced by this aspect provide fertile ground for learning. It is by developing these interests that one can grow intellectually and derive self-satisfaction from mental accomplishments. If natal Mercury is afflicted, it is especially important to growth that the individual take advantage of opportune circumstances revealed by this aspect, for these avenues offer the means of overcoming innate mental blocks. Fruitful ideas come to one during the effective period of this aspect, a period that is particularly helpful to students, writers and others involved in intellectual pursuits.

Transiting Solar Eclipse Square Natal Mercury. The danger with this square lies in the tendency to become overly opinionated, to express ideas too authoritatively.

Egotistical attitudes hamper the reasoning process. Speech and actions, motivated by the urge to prove that one's views are correct and, perhaps the only ideas worth consideration, frequently attract intellectual resistance from associates rather than intelligent feedback. It is important to growth that the individual develop objective thinking habits and open the mind to a broad spectrum of ideas rather than stick to rigid and narrow concepts. This aspect suggests the potential for events that expose mental barriers and produce revealing intellectual experiences. The individual may be indirectly influenced by experiences encountered by a brother or sister during the period of eclipse influence.

Transiting Solar Eclipse Trine Natal Mercury. This trine reveals avenues and relationships that provide ego satisfaction and promote intellectual expression and development. It produces a climate that generates useful ideas plus the confidence to express them and to act on them. This aspect also identifies constructive channels for release of energies created by solar eclipse afflictions and points to ways of dealing with associated problems.

Transiting Solar Eclipse Quincunx Natal Mercury. With this aspect operating in a horoscope, full development of solar eclipse potentials depends upon the correction of negative mental attitudes that retard related affairs. Too, situations that revolve around this quincunx point to the possibility of a karmic sibling relationship, although the relationship may involve a brother or sister from a prior incarnation rather than a sibling belonging to the current lifetime. Events associated with this aspect leave strong mental impressions and contain karmic lessons.

Transiting Solar Eclipse Opposite Natal Mercury. This opposition generates much mental tension and in so doing creates awareness of the importance of thinking for oneself. One becomes more intellectually discriminating and is less likely to accept popular ideas at face value. A positive response to this aspect produces creative thinking and confident decisions that advance affairs influenced by the solar eclipse and natal Mercury. A negative reaction results in nervous tension and frivolous ideas that deter progress. This opposition has a separative effect which is reflected in the events with which it is associated. Experiential possibilities include the release of detrimental mental attitudes, the abandonment of faulty communication habits, the estrangement of a sibling and/or losses connected with solar eclipse/Mercury activities.

TRANSITING SOLAR ECLIPSE ASPECTS TO NATAL VENUS

Transiting solar eclipse aspects to natal Venus bear upon financial matters, partnership interests (marital and/or business) and receptive sexual drives as applicable to Venus' influence in the horoscope. They bring out ego desires associated with beauty and art. Positive reactions enhance sociability and charm; negative responses encourage self-indulgence and vanity.

Transiting Solar Eclipse Conjunct Natal Venus. With this aspect in force, one's natural ability to attract cooperation and love is brought into play to support potentials of the solar eclipse and to further affairs of the house occupied by the conjunction. Social and/or financial influence, as it pertains to these affairs, can be utilized advantageously. This aspect heralds events that entail partnerships, compromise or commitment involving the affairs it influences in accordance with natal and progressed indications. For example, if the conjunction occupies the seventh house and horoscope potentials agree, a single person might marry or become engaged. Under similar astrological circumstances, a married person might enter a business partnership. A second house conjunction might involve a financial merger; a fifth house conjunction, a romantic liaison.

Transiting Solar Eclipse Sextile Natal Venus. This aspect fosters an advantageous atmosphere which attracts good opportunities. Helpful relationships and beneficial situations spring up in the affairs it influences. The individual derives a sense of pleasure and self-satisfaction from these affairs and is, therefore, drawn toward related activities. Financial gains usually accompany advances made in the areas of interest. The happy personal outlook promoted by this aspect does much to help the individual cope with setbacks described by solar eclipse afflictions to other parts of the horoscope.

Transiting Solar Eclipse Square Natal Venus. Extravagance, self-indulgence and conceit create stumbling blocks in the affairs influenced by this square. It emphasizes any hedonistic tendencies shown in the natal horoscope. If the individual does not strive to maintain proper perspective in affairs energized by this aspect, pleasure-seeking becomes the primary objective of ego drives. This aspect suggests experiences that enable one to recognize and overcome self-centeredness and vanity. Related events often center around female friends and relatives or, in a man's horoscope, a spouse or lover.

Transiting Solar Eclipse Trine Natal Venus. This trine promises a flourishing period and happy outcome for affairs with which it is associated. Harmonious relationships smooth the course of progress. Interests influenced by this aspect provide beneficial avenues for release of frustrations and conflicts generated by concurrent solar eclipse afflictions. The period of eclipse influence is a most favorable time to successfully deal with natal afflictions to Venus.

Transiting Solar Eclipse Quincunx Natal Venus. This quincunx focuses on relationships. It suggests the need to change one's attitudes toward companions and associates involved in the affairs it influences. The individual may dominate or be dominated by the relationships in question; either way, lack of balance in relationships impedes growth. Responsibility for improving these relationships, many of which are karmic in nature, rests with the individual. Events that stem from this aspect center around karmic relationship problems.

Transiting Solar Eclipse Opposite Natal Venus. This aspect identifies discordant relationships that interfere with self-development. It alerts the individual to potential resistance from associates and also urges that he or she bring harmony to these situations and/or break off unproductive relationships. Negligence and careless action hinder development and often create financial losses associated with affairs influenced by this opposition. Events linked to this aspect, separative in nature, produce a sense of loss. Alienation of a loved one or financial drain can occur during the period of eclipse influence.

TRANSITING SOLAR ECLIPSE ASPECTS TO NATAL MARS

A transiting solar eclipse aspect to natal Mars motivates. It directs ambition, incentive and one's natural physical drives into the affairs it influences. Because solar eclipse/natal Mars aspects stimulate dynamic physical expression, one can achieve dramatic progress during the period of eclipse influence if energies are utilized constructively. If the solar eclipse and natal Mars are heavily afflicted, reaction is usually headstrong and rash, sometimes violent and brutal.

Transiting Solar Eclipse Conjunct Natal Mars. This conjunction leads to new beginnings and adventurous undertakings in the affairs it energizes. While it is in force, Martian energy, initiative and desire drives add impetus to solar eclipse action in accordance with sign expression and natal potentials. This aspect brings out competitiveness and daring; it prods one to take risks he or she might otherwise avoid. It is important to one's development during the period of influence that energies be carefully controlled and channeled into productive activities. If the conjunction is afflicted, fire, shootings or other Mars-type mishaps are possible.

Transiting Solar Eclipse Sextile Natal Mars. This sextile generates self-confidence; it indicates promising circumstances and opportune avenues that encourage fruitful development of solar eclipse potentials. Energies stimulated by solar eclipse afflictions can be channeled constructively into affairs influenced by the sextile. Unless the horoscope contains conflicting statements, the individual benefits from strong vitality and is well able to meet physical demands of the period.

Transiting Solar Eclipse Square Natal Mars. The period during which this square is in effect can be physically depleting. One tends to be overly active and aggressive. It is difficult, especially for the naturally dynamic person, to pace one's energies in order to avoid exhausting physical resources. This aspect fosters willfulness and argumentativeness which, in turn, often cause setbacks and sometimes lead to accidents. Too, it brings out natural sexual aggressiveness.

Transiting Solar Eclipse Trine Natal Mars. The natural drives symbolic of Mars can be readily utilized to support solar eclipse potentials while this aspect operates. It softens the potential discord and anger associated with Mars and gives positive direction to one's energies. It produces a climate that builds self-confidence and emphasizes natural leadership qualities. It reveals circumstances and affairs that offer least resistance to one's efforts, thus assuring relatively smooth progress for associated interests.

Transiting Solar Eclipse Quincunx Natal Mars. This aspect denotes areas in which natural physical drives are misdirected or misused. It calls attention to the importance of correct utilization of physical energies and the necessity of proper care of the body. It indicates the need to modify aggressive tactics and to alter self-centered attitudes in conducting affairs it influences. The thrust of events associated with this aspect focuses on karmic debts created by anger and rash impulses. Relationships described by this quincunx are those involving male relatives and friends or, in a woman's horoscope, her husband or lover.

Transiting Solar Eclipse Opposite Natal Mars. This opposition reveals physical drives associated with natal Mars that conflict with ego drives described by the solar eclipse. The individual must come to terms with the desire nature as it relates to the ego. For the highly ambitious or overly sexed person, situations generated by this aspect are especially difficult to handle, for it promotes aggression and the tendency to ride roughshod over others. This is a "might is right" aspect that, without easy aspects through which to channel energies productively, often leads to enmity and violence. Events associated with this opposition usually stem from ruthlessness, lack of self-control or hostility.

TRANSITING SOLAR ECLIPSE ASPECTS TO NATAL JUPITER

An aspect between a transiting solar eclipse and natal Jupiter awakens the abundant promise of Jupiter as reflected in the natal horoscope in accordance with the nature of the aspect. One's ethical and moral values undergird the developmental process involving affairs influenced by natal Jupiter and the solar eclipse. A positive response promotes generosity and success; a negative reaction fosters excesses and extravagance.

Transiting Solar Eclipse Conjunct Natal Jupiter. This aspect generates self-confidence, optimism and benevolence. One's principles and integrity represent guiding factors in solar eclipse activity. A heavily afflicted conjunction warns that inflated self-importance and self-aggrandizement stand in the way of growth. If such tendencies are shown in the natal horoscope, the eclipse period of influence is a favorable time to strive for less egotistical attitudes. Regardless of afflictions, benefits (spiritual or material or both) usually accrue during the period. Events associated with this aspect relate to material successes, educational accomplishments or, in a woman's chart, marriage if other factors in the chart agree. Winnings from speculative activities can manifest if the conjunction is exact, well aspected and connected with the natal fifth house or its ruler.

Transiting Solar Eclipse Sextile Natal Jupiter. This sextile accompanies a buoyant period during which one's efforts in related affairs attract rewards. It fosters conditions in which these affairs flourish. One can expect abundant opportunities for expansion in the sphere of interest. If the aspect is connected with the natal tenth house, a promotion or the achievement of a major career goal is likely. In any case, it is associated with progress and success. Educational activities, legal pursuits and/or extensive travel can contribute to development of solar eclipse potentials during the period of eclipse activity.

Transiting Solar Eclipse Square Natal Jupiter. This aspect encourages excesses in the affairs it influences, excesses that cause self-created obstacles. Detrimental practices and attitudes such as gluttony, overindulgence, extravagance and complacency are apt to manifest if the potential is contained in the natal horoscope. It is important to the individual's progress during the eclipse period that he or she curb harmful excesses, strive for moderation and not overextend himself/herself in the affairs influenced by this square. While this aspect is in force, one is frequently confronted by learning experiences that teach benevolence, integrity and temperance and encounters events created by personal excesses or extravagance.

Transiting Solar Eclipse Trine Natal Jupiter. A sense of general well-being fosters optimism and self-confidence throughout the period during which this trine is in effect. The promising atmosphere and positive self-attitudes that prevail at the time enable one to shed self-imposed limitations that stem from personal insecurities and low self-esteem. The individual, able to function at best under these helpful circumstances, can achieve worthwhile objectives in the affairs influenced by this aspect and attain a high level of self-development in accordance with natal and solar eclipse potentials.

Transiting Solar Eclipse Quincunx Natal Jupiter. This quincunx identifies ethical and/or religious attitudes that slant moral and spiritual development. There may be biases present which color abstract thought, limit intellectual expansion and erode affairs influenced by the eclipse and natal Jupiter. Relationships with in-laws, persons of foreign birth and the clergy should be examined for karmic implications. Experiences of a profound religious/spiritual nature correspond to this aspect.

Transiting Solar Eclipse Opposite Natal Jupiter. This opposition brings out egotistical tendencies and pompous attitudes. The drive for self-satisfaction frequently leads one to overestimate his or her potentials. Losses in affairs influenced by this aspect occur as result of unwise expansion prompted by self-centered attributes and faulty perspectives. Too, smugness, indolence and self-indulgence interfere with the progress of interests associated with the eclipse and natal Jupiter. Experiences and events associated with this aspect produce awareness of lack of self-objectivity and encourage realistic self-appraisal, thus contributing to development of balanced self-perspective.

TRANSITING SOLAR ECLIPSE ASPECTS TO NATAL SATURN

Comparatively slow progress characterizes the effective period of a transiting solar eclipse/natal Saturn aspect. Situations that teach patience, self-discipline and self-reliance develop during the period. Vitality may be somewhat lower than normal, and persons who suffer from chronic ailments should be particularly careful to follow prescribed medical procedures. Events that occur in connection with hard solar eclipse/natal Saturn aspects have lasting consequences.

Transiting Solar Eclipse Conjunct Natal Saturn. This conjunction stirs awareness of one's responsibilities in the affairs and relationships it influences. A realistic approach and constructive endeavors promote development of solar eclipse potentials. If the conjunction is afflicted, self-doubts and lack of confidence impede progress. Experiences associated with this aspect are those which have enduring implications; they often involve older persons, the father or other authority figure or, in a woman's horoscope, the husband. A turning point in one's career or other major milestone can occur if a progressed planet or transit triggers the potential of an exact conjunction.

Transiting Solar Eclipse Sextile Natal Saturn. The climate generated by this aspect is somewhat sobering; nevertheless, it fosters a realistic self-image and encourages controlled action. It promotes caution, self-restraint and conservatism but not to the degree that these attitudes bar progress. Opportunities that arise during the period in which this sextile is effective permit one to make steady strides toward objectives associated with related affairs.

Transiting Solar Eclipse Square Natal Saturn. Obstacles suggested by this square are those rooted in lack of self-discipline or low self-esteem. Fear of failure and excessive caution can literally paralyze self-expression. It is important to development of solar eclipse potentials that the individual recognize personal failings and put them in proper perspective. It is essential that one not allow negative attributes to overshadow positive qualities. The period during which this aspect is in effect can be a trying time fraught with delays and heavy responsibilities in the affairs it influences. Events and experiences associated with this square teach patience and perseverance.

Transiting Solar Eclipse Trine Natal Saturn. This trine introduces the kind of atmosphere that helps the individual master problems rooted in irresponsibility and lack of self-discipline. One gains a realistic view of his or her role in affairs influenced by this aspect. The period during which it is effective, a stable one unmarked by extreme highs or lows, usually produces substantial development of solar eclipse potentials, development that reflects enduring qualities associated with Saturn.

Transiting Solar Eclipse Quincunx Natal Saturn. This aspect points out defeatist attitudes and other characteristics such as ultra-conservatism and low self-esteem that hinder growth. It calls for more positive attitudes toward the affairs and relationships it influences. This quincunx carries karmic connotations. It marks a time of reckoning that demands payment of karmic debts accrued in the past. Older persons, the father or, in a woman's horoscope, the husband play important roles in events associated with this aspect.

Transiting Solar Eclipse Opposite Natal Saturn. This opposition releases potentials of natal Saturn, but it also generates resistance that hampers development of solar eclipse potentials. It is essential to growth that one maintain a careful balance between practical interests associated with natal Saturn and self-needs described by the solar eclipse. A prudent sense of personal responsibility does much to assist progress in affairs influenced by this aspect. Loss of prestige and experiences that undermine self-confidence can occur if natal Saturn or the solar eclipse is severely afflicted. Failures and other ego-deflating events often accompany this opposition.

TRANSITING SOLAR ECLIPSE ASPECTS TO NATAL URANUS

Aspects to natal Uranus from transiting solar eclipses emphasize innovative attitudes and natural ingenuity. They often herald refreshing changes and new vistas. One's humanitarian instincts and interest in social causes develop more fully during the period of aspect influence. Positive responses to solar eclipse/natal Uranus aspects put one in touch with contemporary trends; negative reactions promote radical proclivities.

Transiting Solar Eclipse Conjunct Natal Uranus. This conjunction announces a vibrant period during which one experiences the desire to explore unusual avenues of interest and is attracted to the exotic. One derives ego satisfaction through humanitarian efforts directed into affairs energized by this aspect. Group pursuits play a leading role in development of solar eclipse potentials. This aspect, directly associated with sudden events, hastens activity linked to concurrent solar eclipse aspects. If the conjunction is afflicted, related events and experiences reflect the bizarre, eccentric, disruptive qualities characteristic of Uranus.

Transiting Solar Eclipse Sextile Natal Uranus. The magnetic atmosphere that surrounds affairs influenced by this sextile attracts unusual opportunities best described as the "once in a lifetime" variety. The magic of the period wakens within even the most conservative individual a sense of the avant-garde. One experiences a pull toward the different and the unconventional. This aspect generates pride in originality of creative self-expression.

Transiting Solar Eclipse Square Natal Uranus. This aspect brings out any radical or eccentric tendencies contained in the natal horoscope. It warns the individual against continuing willful and rebellious practices that block progress or contribute to erratic development. The wise individual will prepare for contingencies associated with the affairs influenced by this square, for this aspect involves the unexpected and frequently heralds ego-shattering events.

Transiting Solar Eclipse Trine Natal Uranus. Change and experimentation are encouraged during the effective period of this aspect. Novel circumstances appear, and different interests attract. Changing conditions and unfamiliar situations add color and appeal to affairs influenced by this trine. It fosters a refreshing outlook and unbiased views. Humanitarian tendencies that contribute to self-development flourish under this aspect.

Transiting Solar Eclipse Quincunx Natal Uranus. This quincunx specifies the need to modify radical tendencies and personal idiosyncracies described in the natal horoscope. It advises modification of non-conformist behavior and rebellious attitudes. It is sometimes associated with group karma, although in any case it carries personal karmic implications associated with affairs and relationships it influences. Experiences that accompany this aspect teach lessons relating to brotherhood and universal love.

Transiting Solar Eclipse Opposite Natal Uranus. The energy generated by this aspect urges one to confront the situations and affairs influenced by the solar eclipse and natal Uranus. One is alerted to stagnant and unproductive courses of action and motivated to make changes. Extraordinary improvements can be made during the period this opposition is in effect. However, negative reaction produces changes that stem from little more than discontent, the desire for something different. Such changes usually conflict with one's best interests and result in little, if any, constructive advancement. Events that correlate to this aspect introduce unfamiliar sets of circumstances with which one must deal. These situations call for ingenuity and innovation.

TRANSITING SOLAR ECLIPSE ASPECTS TO NATAL NEPTUNE

Transiting solar eclipse aspects to natal Neptune awaken interest in spiritual matters and arouse imaginative faculties. They also stir latent psychic proclivities. A positive reaction gains spiritual enlightenment and recognition of illusionary beliefs; a negative response lends to self-delusion and escapism.

Transiting Solar Eclipse Conjunct Natal Neptune. This conjunction brings hidden matters to attention. The individual senses a need for inner examination in order to gain self-understanding. Obscure motives and/or karmic responsibilities come to light. Much spiritual progress can be achieved during the eclipse period of influence since events associated with this aspect frequently open doors to spiritual growth. Self-delusion and the desire to escape responsibilities in matters influenced by this aspect often accompany a heavily afflicted solar eclipse/natal Neptune conjunction. In this case, related experiences can involve alcohol, drugs and subterfuge.

Transiting Solar Eclipse Sextile Natal Neptune. While this aspect is in force, solar eclipse activity reflects the sensitivity and compassion shown by Neptune in the natal horoscope. One has opportunities to direct imagination and creativity into the affairs influenced by the solar eclipse and natal Neptune. This sextile is especially helpful to persons engaged in Neptunian arts and those who have psychic ability. It also encourages one to seek spiritual guidance.

Transiting Solar Eclipse Square Natal Neptune. This square generates chaos and confusion. It is up to the individual to discriminate between the real and the unreal. Fantasy, drugs, alcohol, cultism, and other forms of Neptunian escapism represent blocks to progress as do delusions about one's own importance and capabilities. Experiences associated with this aspect strip away one's illusions and delusions. Frequently, events that accompany it stem from fraud or other types of deception.

Transiting Solar Eclipse Trine Natal Neptune. A dreamy quality that contributes to spiritual and creative inspiration characterizes the aura surrounding affairs influenced by this trine, but unless a hard aspect operates simultaneously to promote ambition, little may come of one's visions. Relationships and situations associated with this aspect contribute to creative self-expression, spiritual unfoldment and psychic development.

Transiting Solar Eclipse Quincunx Natal Neptune. This aspect identifies karmic responsibilities involving relationships associated with the affairs it influences. It signals the need to rectify past wrongs. People who come into one's life for the first time while this quincunx is in effect frequently share karmic ties with the individual. Comparison of the individual's horoscope with that of another person will reveal whether or not a karmic relationship exists. An event that stems from this aspect stamps the karmic wheel for better or worse depending upon one's reaction to and action in the situation.

Transiting Solar Eclipse Opposite Natal Neptune. An individual can make much spiritual and karmic progress during the period in which this aspect operates, for it alerts one to spiritual and karmic needs. One who responds negatively tends to disregard this signal by burying his or her head in the sand, so to speak. By refusing to face realities in situations energized by this opposition, one places ego needs in direct conflict with spiritual needs. A self-centered course of action is a self-destructive one that not only stands in the way of self-development but also leads to spiritual downfall. Events associated with this aspect are the sort one brings upon himself/herself, rewarding or otherwise, as results of past actions.

TRANSITING SOLAR ECLIPSE ASPECTS TO NATAL PLUTO.

A solar eclipse aspect to natal Pluto activates the evolutionary process symbolic of Pluto. It has a transforming effect which enables one to overcome handicaps that surface during the period of effectiveness and turn adversities to advantage. Easy solar eclipse/natal Pluto aspects enable one to draw upon universal prana which rejuvenates physically and spiritually, increasing vitality, recuperative powers and spiritual strength. A negative response evokes cruelty and inhumane tendencies if such exist in the natal horoscope.

Transiting Solar Eclipse Conjunct Natal Pluto. A power aspect, this conjunction brings out the forceful side of one's nature. It is accompanied by an overwhelming desire to fully control the affairs it influences. Domination of these interests and other people involved in them becomes a matter of self-respect. Whether the individual acts overtly or in a less obtrusive manner to gain dominance depends upon the sign the conjunction occupies and natal potentials, but regardless of the route taken, the objective of action is the same - to achieve power. Events associated with this aspect rejuvenate related situations and transform one's attitudes regarding these affairs. In a man's chart, sexual potency increases. If the conjunction is afflicted, the individual may encounter degrading experiences; if criminal tendencies exist in the natal horoscope, they are apt to manifest.

Transiting Solar Eclipse Sextile Natal Pluto. This sextile produces opportune circumstances that enable the individual to exercise leadership in the affairs influenced by the solar eclipse and natal Pluto and to direct these interests along the course he or she chooses. These interests offer avenues that lead to spiritual evolvement as well as to self-development. This aspect also increases vitality and enhances recuperative powers.

Transiting Solar Eclipse Square Natal Pluto. This square arouses strong ambition and a great deal of dissatisfaction with the prevailing state of affairs it influences. One's ego drives center on transforming these affairs according to his or her will. Properly channeled, the energy created by this aspect can be constructively utilized to master the self. A negative response brings out ruthlessness, and the individual may resort to coercive tactics in order to gain the upper hand in related affairs. Events that accompany this aspect, usually traumatic in nature unless the orb is wide, produce fundamental changes in the sphere of influence and in one's spiritual attitudes.

Transiting Solar Eclipse Trine Natal Pluto. Insight into spiritual matters and spiritual unfoldment come under the influence of this trine. It also gives positive direction to solar eclipse/natal Pluto energies enabling one to achieve much progress and growth along lines of self-improvement and self-development through the affairs and relationships it energizes. The individual can control the affairs influenced by this aspect without attracting animosity or resorting to coercion.

Transiting Solar Eclipse Quincunx Natal Pluto. This aspect brings to light conditions having to do with past, present and future incarnations. It gives insight into matters concerning life, death, and life after death. It yields clues to past mistakes, indicates present karmic responsibilities and points to steps to be taken prior to the next reincarnation. By making positive adjustments in attitudes and actions concerning the affairs, situations and relationships influenced by this aspect, one can acquire material as well as spiritual gains. Events associated with this quincunx deal with the meaning of physical and spiritual resurrection.

Transiting Solar Eclipse Opposite Natal Pluto. This opposition creates a strong desire to exercise authority and gain power in related affairs. The very nature of the aspect suggests that one can expect to encounter resistance to efforts directed toward these ends. The important thing here is how one deals with opposition and conflict. The use of physical force and/or other means of intimidation creates greater problems that jeopardize one's interests and threaten self-development. By utilizing the insight that accompanies this aspect, one can penetrate the depths of conflicts and find the means of turning these situations around. Depending upon potentials revealed in the natal horoscope, events associated with this aspect carry spiritual or physical impact or both.

TRANSITING SOLAR ECLIPSE ASPECTS TO NATAL MOON'S NODES

A transiting solar eclipse that aspects the natal Moon's North Node simultaneously forms a complementary aspect with its South Node. Interpretations given below include both the current experiential patterns symbolic of the natal North Node and the karmic implications of the natal South Node.

Transiting Solar Eclipse Conjunct Natal North Node Opposite Natal South Node. Solar eclipse potentials focus upon affairs of the house occupied by the eclipse and the natal North Node, and it is through these interests that self-development primarily rests. The opposite house, occupied by the natal South Node, can draw upon solar eclipse energies to clear away karmic limitations described by the natal South Node and, therefore, these affairs can be more fully developed. Events associated with these aspects, cyclic in nature, contain repeated lessons unlearned in the past, the final lesson in a series of related lessons or the initial lesson in a new path to self-understanding.

Transiting Solar Eclipse Conjunct Natal South Node Opposite Natal North Node. Self-centered tendencies surface during the period these aspects are effective. They reveal egotistical attitudes associated with the natal South Node which have created handicaps in the past and presently conflict with positive experiential potentials described by the natal North Node. The self-awareness fostered by these aspects contributes to the capacity to develop selfless attributes that promote personal growth and reinforce constructive solar eclipse activity. Events that manifest under this configuration stem from selfish action, action which the individual perpetrates or action of which he or she is the victim.

Transiting Solar Eclipse Sextile Natal North Node Trine Natal South Node. These aspects generate opportunities for positive growth experiences associated with the natal North Node. They also encourage one to master detrimental karmic tendencies symbolized by the natal South Node. Constructive self-development and karmic progress characterize the period during which these aspects operate. They play a contributory role in solar eclipse activity in other areas of eclipse influence in the horoscope.

Transiting Solar Eclipse Sextile Natal South Node Trine Natal North Node. Karmic responsibilities described by the natal South Node come to light under the influence of these aspects. These revelations represent opportunities to erase spiritual debts;however, it is up to the individual to utilize the knowledge constructively. These aspects also put one in touch with current trends and foster socially acceptable attitudes in affairs influenced by the solar eclipse and natal North Node.

Transiting Solar Eclipse Square Natal North Node Square Natal South Node. This configuration places the solar eclipse at the focal point of a T-square involving both natal nodes. This T-square describes obstacles created by personal attitudes that are incongruous with prevailing thought (natal North Node) and blocks associated with karmic limitations (natal South Node). Responsibility for removing these barriers rests with the individual who can utilize the affairs, situations and relationships influenced by the solar eclipse to do so. Experiences that accompany these aspects contain lessons that promote self-development and contribute to karmic progress.

Transiting Solar Eclipse Square Natal South Node Square Natal North Node. See "Transiting Solar Eclipse Square Natal North Node Square Natal South Node."

Transiting Solar Eclipse Trine Natal North Node Sextile Natal South Node. See "Transiting Solar Eclipse Sextile Natal South Node Trine Natal North Node."

Transiting Solar Eclipse Trine Natal South Node Sextile Natal North Node. See *"Transiting Solar Eclipse Sextile Natal North Node Trine Natal South Node."*

Transiting Solar Eclipse Quincunx Natal North Node Semi-sextile Natal South Node. These aspects indicate that the individual is out of harmony with affairs of the house occupied by the natal North Node and tends to be hemmed in by the past in relation to the house occupied by the natal South Node. Affairs influenced by the solar eclipse provide the basis for understanding contemporary thought (natal North Node) and ridding oneself of negative karmic proclivities (natal South Node) in order that self-development can proceed unimpeded in these areas and solar eclipse potentials can be fully utilized. Events associated with these aspects teach lessons that unite the past with the present.

Transiting Solar Eclipse Quincunx Natal South Node Semi-sextile Natal North Node. These aspects signal the need to reform selfish habits associated with the natal South Node in order to progress karmically and to fully develop solar eclipse potentials. Positive utilization of experiential trends described by the natal North Node contributes to development in areas influenced by both nodes and the solar eclipse. Events that accompany these aspects carry karmic significance and have strong impact upon the inner nature.

Transiting Solar Eclipse Opposite Natal North Node Conjunct Natal South Node. See *"Transiting Solar Eclipse Conjunct Natal South Node Opposite Natal North Node."*

Transiting Solar Eclipse Opposite Natal South Node Conjunct Natal North Node. See *Transiting Solar Eclipse Conjunct Natal North Node Opposite Natal South Node."*

TRANSITING SOLAR ECLIPSE ASPECTS TO THE NATAL ASCENDANT AND NATAL DESCENDENT

When a transiting solar eclipse aspects the Ascendant of a horoscope, it also forms a complementary aspect with the Descendant. These aspects bear a very personal connotation through influence on the Ascendant which is combined with relationship needs as described by the Descendant.

Transiting Solar Eclipse Conjunct Natal Ascendant Opposite Natal Descendant. These aspects foster self-development by arousing self-awareness and encouraging personal expression. Self-identify becomes important to ego satisfaction during the period of eclipse influence. The period is one in which a person desires to be accepted for himself/herself as an individual. If the Ascendant is severely afflicted, arrogance may displace humility or defeatism supplant confidence depending upon the nature of the afflictions and the planets involved; many persons undergo a decline in physical energy. Increased vitality is characteristic if the Ascendant is well-aspected. Experiences associated with these aspects bear much personal significance. Self-enriching experiences or personal achievements often manifest under these aspects or, at the other end of the spectrum, personal defeat or estrangement depending upon horoscope potentials and one's reaction to solar eclipse energies.

Transiting Solar Eclipse Conjunct Natal Descendant Opposite Natal Ascendant. The period during which these aspects are effective produces awareness of the roles other people play in one's life and vice versa. Personal growth depends upon one's capacity to establish and maintain fruitful, satisfying relationships. Usually, the individual attempts to form ties that enhance self-esteem. These aspects correlate to events that entail a personal commitment such as marriage or formation of a business partnership. If the solar eclipse or angles are afflicted and natal potentials agree, one may experience separation, divorce or the dissolution of a partnership.

Transiting Solar Eclipse Sextile Natal Ascendant Trine Natal Descendant. These aspects engender personal opportunities and harmonious relationships. The individual is readily accepted by others and attracts benefits through social interaction. Personal efforts and cooperative endeavors both contribute to growth and reinforce development of solar eclipse potentials. These aspects do much to mitigate the impact of events associated with concurrent hard solar eclipse aspects.

Transiting Solar Eclipse Sextile Natal Descendant Trine Natal Ascendant. These aspects produce a harmonious atmosphere in which, because the individual projects a likeable image, beneficial relationships flourish. Opportunities to advance personal purposes and to more fully develop solar eclipse potentials arise through seventh house affiliations. These favorable circumstances promote personal growth and fulfilling relationships; they also provide constructive outlets for energies created by solar eclipse afflictions.

Transiting Solar Eclipse Square Natal Ascendant Square Natal Descendant. These aspects, which form a T-square, usually place the solar eclipse near one of the vertical angles (MC or IC). It is through the affairs directly influenced by the solar eclipse that one must channel personal efforts and draw upon supportive relationships if solar eclipse potentials are to be fully realized. Obstacles inherent in these squares stem from egotistical attitudes and inadequate relationships. Events associated with these aspects are usually rooted in the inability to correctly evaluate affairs influenced by the solar eclipse and in the failure to relate harmoniously to others involved in attendant situations. Related experiences reveal personal biases and negative social attitudes that inhibit self-development.

Transiting Solar Eclipse Square Natal Descendant Square Natal Ascendant. See *"Transiting Solar Eclipse Square Natal Ascendant Square Natal Descendant."*

Transiting Solar Eclipse Trine Natal Ascendant Sextile Natal Descendant. See *"Transiting Solar Eclipse Sextile Natal Descendant Trine Natal Ascendant."*

Transiting Solar Eclipse Trine Natal Descendant Sextile Natal Ascendant. See *"Transiting Solar Eclipse Sextile Natal Ascendant Trine Natal Descendant."*

Transiting Solar Eclipse Quincunx Natal Ascendant Semi-sextile Natal Descendant. These aspects point to character flaws that hinder self-development and hamper success in affairs activated by the solar eclipse. The individual can look to associates (primarily seventh house relationships) for the support and encouragement he or she needs to effect and sustain needed personality adjustments. Events associated with this configuration usually reveal some facet of personal karma and often result from misdirected personal action.

Transiting Solar Eclipse Quincunx Natal Descendant Semi-sextile Natal Ascendant. This aspect arrangement points to lack of cooperation - either the failure to cooperate with others or the failure to obtain cooperation from others - as the essential contributory factor in unsatisfactory seventh house relationships. The individual may see associates as being either too competitive or too yielding or vice versa. It is important that the individual emphasize personality traits that balance cooperative tendencies with the competitive spirit. Experiences associated with these aspects reveal karmic relationships; it is through affairs influenced by the solar eclipse that mutual karmic problems can be worked out.

Transiting Solar Eclipse Opposite Natal Ascendant Conjunct Natal Descendant. See *"Transiting Solar Eclipse Conjunct Natal Descendant Opposite Natal Ascendant."*

Transiting Solar Eclipse Opposite Natal Descendant Conjunct Natal Ascendant. See *"Transiting Solar Eclipse Conjunct Natal Ascendant Opposite Natal Descendant."*

TRANSITING SOLAR ECLIPSE ASPECTS TO THE NATAL MIDHEAVEN AND NATAL IMUM COELI (NADIR)

An aspect to the natal Midheaven (MC) and its simultaneous aspect to the natal Imum Coeli (IC) deal with worldly ambitions and family affairs and their influence in self-development during the period of eclipse effectiveness.

Transiting Solar Eclipse Conjunct Natal MC Opposite Natal IC. The drive to make one's mark in the world, to achieve professional prominence, to gain career stature predominates the period during which the solar eclipse activates the horoscope. Family interests usually assume secondary status throughout the period, although the wise individual will draw upon family relationships to support and encourage worldly ambitions. Because one takes inordinate pride in worldly accomplishments and derives great ego satisfaction from his or her achievements, the period contains potentials for tremendous career advancement, potentials for success that contribute to self-development. An afflicted solar eclipse/MC conjunction points to possible setbacks and advises cautionary moves as described in the horoscope. Events associated with an exact configuration do not always bear directly upon the career or the domestic sphere, but they do have tremendous impact and usually indicate a major turning point in life. Related experiences may involve the father or persons of high rank.

Transiting Solar Eclipse Conjunct Natal IC Opposite Natal MC. Primary activity of the period during which these aspects are effective reflects the pride one takes in home and family. Usually, one tries to make the living quarters more comfortable or move to a different home that is more suitable to his/her lifestyle; too, one attempts to enhance the quality of family life. These aspects also alert one to imbalances that exist between worldly interests and family aims. Experiences that manifest as result of these aspects usually affect the career or family and frequently involve one of the parents.

Transiting Solar Eclipse Sextile Natal MC Trine Natal IC. The promising climate generated by these aspects attracts career opportunities and fosters a supportive home atmosphere. The period during which eclipse activity is effective carries the potential for strong advances in one's chosen field. If other factors in the horoscope agree, a change in career directions is possible. Family support of one's worldly ambitions, usually obvious throughout the period, is, of course, helpful.

Transiting Solar Eclipse Sextile Natal IC Trine Natal MC. These aspects produce a harmonious rapport between career and family concerns. These interests contribute to development of affairs of the house occupied by the solar eclipse. Often, family influence has much to do with the substantial opportunities one receives during the period of eclipse influence. Too, important professional contacts also prove beneficial. The period usually reflects warm family relationships and comparatively rapid career progress.

Transiting Solar Eclipse Square Natal MC Square Natal IC. Completing a T-square formation with the solar eclipse at the focal point (frequently near one of the horizontal angles - Ascendant or Descendant), these aspects identify public/career and family interests that block affairs of the house occupied by the solar eclipse and vice versa. Self-development hinges upon one's capacity to channel supportive fourth and tenth house activity through solar eclipse energies. It is important that one draw upon positive attributes of related affairs and utilize helpful situations. These aspects are associated with events which thwart advancement of solar eclipse potentials and impede self-development. Growth depends upon one's ability to master such obstacles.

Transiting Solar Eclipse Square Natal IC Square Natal MC. See *"Transiting Solar Eclipse Square Natal MC Square Natal IC."*

Transiting Solar Eclipse Trine Natal MC Sextile Natal IC. See *"Transiting Solar Eclipse Sextile Natal IC Trine Natal MC."*

Transiting Solar Eclipse Trine Natal IC Sextile Natal MC. See *"Transiting Solar Eclipse Sextile Natal MC Trine Natal IC."*

Transiting Solar Eclipse Quincunx Natal MC Semi-sextile Natal IC. These aspects signify the need to reevaluate worldly goals. It is essential to self-development and to the progress of affairs influenced by this configuration that one identify courses not right for him or her and discontinue them. The period during which these aspects are effective fosters changes of direction, and associated events usually effect such changes. Relaxation of family pressures and a fairly harmonious home atmosphere enable the individual to direct proper attention to other purposes important during the period.

Transiting Solar Eclipse Quincunx Natal IC Semi-sextile Natal MC. These aspects suggest that negative attitudes and fruitless activities which center around home and family affairs obstruct development of solar eclipse potentials. The tendency to be selfish with family members or to dominate family life, along with other egotistical inclinations, can be viewed as characteristics that stifle growth and need correction. Events of the period point out problem areas which could benefit from redirection. Career interests and public associations play supportive roles in solar eclipse development.

Transiting Solar Eclipse Opposite Natal MC Conjunct Natal IC. See *"Transiting Solar Eclipse Conjunct Natal IC Opposite Natal MC."*

Transiting Solar Eclipse Opposite Natal IC Conjunct Natal MC. See *"Transiting Solar Eclipse Conjunct Natal MC Opposite Natal IC."*

TRANSITING SOLAR ECLIPSE ASPECTS TO PROGRESSED PLANETS AND ANGLES

The meaning of a solar eclipse aspect to a natal planet or angle can be applied to its progressed counterpart with some modification. Natal and progressed potentials of the progressed planet/angle must be examined and other aspects it forms simultaneously in the horoscope considered. A change from the natal sign or house position places a different orientation on an aspect involving a progressed planet. *Exact* aspects between a solar eclipse and a progressed planet/angle carry the same weight as their natal counterparts; *inexact* aspects do not. If the progressed planet/angle is not activating the horoscope via an exact aspect to a natal point, the effect of its *inexact* aspect with a transiting solar eclipse, although of similar quality as a like natal aspect, will be mild in comparison unless the solar eclipse also aspects the progressed planet's dispositor (planetary ruler in the case of an angle) or a planet/angle with which it formed a natal aspect. If a progressed planet/angle in hard aspect with a solar eclipse reaches the partile point during the eclipse effective period, it usually touches off an eclipse related event at the time.

CHAPTER 6

LUNAR ECLIPSE ASPECTS

The orb for aspects between a transiting lunar eclipse and natal or progressed planets and angles is the same as that for transiting solar eclipse aspects. Lunar eclipse aspects add emotional color to the affairs they energize. Easy aspects identify avenues that can be readily utilized in support of solar eclipse activity; hard aspects point out courses of resistance. Experiences associated with hard aspects leave emotional impressions that influence the drives of planets involved.

TRANSITING LUNAR ECLIPSE ASPECTS TO NATAL SUN

An aspect between a transiting lunar eclipse and the natal Sun awakens feelings and instincts that relate to creative self-expression and all that the Sun represents in the natal horoscope. It arouses inner needs linked to self-needs and individuality. Easy aspects permit free-flowing exchange between emotional energies and ego drives. Hard aspects produce an uneasy emotional/egoistic rapport and expose negative emotional/instinctive patterns that impede natal Sun potentials.

Transiting Lunar Eclipse Conjunct Natal Sun. With this aspect, a lunar eclipse emotionalizes the creative self-expression described by the natal Sun according to qualities of the sign the conjunction occupies and natal potentials. Subconscious motivations foster awareness of self; inner urges prompt outer expression of self drives. Usually, the individual feels good about himself/herself and approaches affairs influenced by this aspect energetically and confidently. If the conjunction is severely afflicted, there can be an enervating effect that weakens natural vitality and lowers self-esteem.

Transiting Lunar Eclipse Sextile Natal Sun. One instinctively channels energies produced by the natal Sun into affairs influenced by this sextile. The period of eclipse influence promotes extensive development of these interests which, in turn, reinforces progress in activities associated with the solar eclipse(s) belonging to the same sequence. The sense of inner satisfaction and general well-being that prevails during the period this aspect is in effect helps one deal with obstacles that frustrate natal Sun and solar eclipse potentials as described by afflictions.

Transiting Lunar Eclipse Square Natal Sun. This aspect brings to light emotional hangups and/or subconscious attitudes that conflict with natal Sun drives and therefore block full development of natal potentials along with those of the solar eclipse(s) in the sequence. Because of feelings of dissatisfaction and uncertainty generated by this square, many people turn away from the affairs it energizes. However, a positive response brings awareness of and resolution to problems identified by this aspect.

Transiting Lunar Eclipse Trine Natal Sun. This trine generates an atmosphere in which the individual feels comfortable and at ease -- in his or her own element, so to speak. Because one's efforts in affairs influenced by this aspect proceed relatively unhampered, the individual gains confidence to reach out into areas influenced by the solar eclipse(s) in the sequence and to utilize lunar eclipse interests in support of solar eclipse development.

Transiting Lunar Eclipse Quincunx Natal Sun. This quincunx identifies subconscious motivations and instinctive reactions that interfere with full development of natal Sun potentials. Corrective measures directed toward the affairs it energizes clear away impediments to natal Sun development and open these avenues to support potentials of the solar eclipse(s) that appear in the same sequence.

Transiting Lunar Eclipse Opposite Natal Sun. This aspect reveals natal Sun potentials the individual has neglected to fully develop. A positive response enables one to overcome aversion to affairs it energizes and to utilize these interests to reinforce solar eclipse potentials. A negative response results in a stagnant situation that does nothing to contribute to development of solar eclipse potentials although it does not hamper progress in areas directly influenced by the solar eclipse(s) in the sequence.

TRANSITING LUNAR ECLIPSE ASPECTS TO NATAL MOON

When a transiting lunar eclipse aspects the natal Moon, it prompts emotional expressiveness and brings out the hidden side of the emotional nature as described in the natal horoscope. It arouses repressed emotions and stirs psychic tendencies. Easy aspects lend to inner security and positive direction of emotional drives. Hard aspects expose negative emotional proclivities and instinctive biases that frustrate growth.

Transiting Lunar Eclipse Conjunct Natal Moon. This aspect promotes outward emotional expression thus enabling one to reach out to others on an emotional level within the context of the sign in which the conjunction occurs according to natal Moon potentials. For the emotionally reticent person, it can be helpful in learning to express inner feelings more openly. The overly emotional may react so strongly that emotional expression is excessive, alternating between extreme highs and lows, especially if the conjunction is afflicted. This aspect also activates subconscious attitudes and dormant psychic faculties. One usually intuitively senses situations pertinent to affairs it influences. Correct utilization of intuition leads to constructive moves that supplement action of the solar eclipse(s) in the sequence. However, depending upon all potentials and particularly if Pisces or Neptune is involved, one must be careful not to be misled by erroneous psychic instincts.

Transiting Lunar Eclipse Sextile Natal Moon. This aspect fosters conditions that encourage emotional expression and promote psychic development. It points to outlets through which one can release emotional blocks and subconscious frustrations described by afflictions to the natal Moon. The avenues this trine influences offer emotional fulfillment and reinforce development of solar eclipse potentials.

Transiting Lunar Eclipse Square Natal Moon. This square calls attention to inner frustrations that block emotional growth and thwart progress in affairs it influences. It signals the need to overcome such handicaps in order to improve these affairs and to utilize lunar energies in positive support of solar eclipse activity. Although this aspect usually curtails outward emotional expression, it is associated with excessive or misdirected displays of sentiment if the potential is contained in the natal horoscope.

Transiting Lunar Eclipse Trine Natal Moon. The inner harmony one experiences during the period this trine is in effect enables that person to maintain an easy rapport with other people involved in the areas influenced. This comfortable atmosphere lends to progress in these affairs and encourages the individual to more fully develop those interests directly influenced by the solar eclipse(s) in the sequence.

Transiting Lunar Eclipse Quincunx Natal Moon. This quincunx reveals inherited emotional traits and instinctive attitudes that inhibit progress in affairs it energizes. It creates inner dissatisfaction and emotional vacillation. Here, growth hinges upon strengthening the inner nature. Positive emotional reactions reinforce solar eclipse activity; negative responses restrain it.

Transiting Lunar Eclipse Opposite Natal Moon. The period during which this opposition is in effect can be emotionally stressful. At the time, the individual grows aware of hidden frustrations and repressed emotional desires with which he or she must deal. The person who reacts negatively to this aspect tends to waste emotional energies by wallowing in self-pity, focusing on emotional insecurities and/or failing to find constructive outlets for inner tensions. One who responds positively channels emotional energies productively to add emotional force to activity in the affairs the aspect influences and to back up solar eclipse potentials.

TRANSITING LUNAR ECLIPSE ASPECTS TO NATAL MERCURY

A transiting lunar eclipse that aspects natal Mercury elicits intuitive and instinctive qualities that are part of the natural intellect. Emotional considerations influence the reasoning process to the degree permitted by natal potentials, and one tends to verbalize feelings more than usual. Easy aspects harmonize emotional and mental qualities. Because one is more intellectually sensitive during the period of aspect influence, communicative abilities and persuasive capabilities improve. Hard aspects, indicative of a stressful period in which feelings and decision making are at odds, produce restlessness, discontent and vacillation.

Transiting Lunar Eclipse Conjunct Natal Mercury. While this aspect is effective, the individual derives great inner satisfaction from intellectual accomplishments and, therefore, tends to pursue intellectually oriented interests associated with affairs influenced by the lunar eclipse and natal Mercury. Unless the conjunction is severely afflicted, associated learning experiences, positive in nature, contribute to development of potentials of the solar eclipse(s) belonging to the same sequence. If the conjunction is heavily afflicted, nervousness and emotional instability manifest. It is difficult for the individual to arrive at decisions that are both sensible and emotionally satisfying. One often has to choose between logic and inner happiness.

Transiting Lunar Eclipse Sextile Natal Mercury. This sextile promotes a beneficial emotional/mental rapport that fosters intuitive and intellectual development. It activates the subconscious, enhances one's sense of timing and contributes to memory improvement. The affairs influenced by this aspect provide fertile ground for learning and expression of ideas. The perspectives one acquires in these affairs support solar eclipse activity.

Transiting Lunar Eclipse Square Natal Mercury. This square reveals subconscious emotional/mental blocks that hamper clear thinking, sound decision-making and the ability to express ideas. It also points out psychological blocks that hinder outward expression of one's feelings. Progress of affairs influenced by the lunar eclipse and Natal Mercury and their reinforcement of solar eclipse activity depends upon a positive approach that demands one recognize and correct biases and negative attitudes which interfere with intellectual and emotional development.

Transiting Lunar Eclipse Trine Natal Mercury. This aspect produces the sort of atmosphere that encourages mental concentration, learning and communication. It is through utilization of one's mental potentials, intuitive faculties and emotional resources that the affairs influenced by this trine can be advantageously developed and employed to reinforce solar eclipse activity. This aspect also contributes to memory improvement, common sense, intellectual versatility and sensitivity to the feelings and ideas of others within the dicates of signs involved and natal potentials.

Transiting Lunar Eclipse Quincunx Natal Mercury. This quincunx describes subconscious motivations and inborn mental traits that frustrate growth. It also reveals emotional inhibitions and mental quirks acquired during early upbringing. It heralds an introspective period that encourages one to identify and change negative mental/emotional attitudes. It calls for objective examination of the mental and emotional natures, and it promises progress in the affairs it influences once corrective steps are taken. Otherwise, these affairs proceed slowly and are useless to solar eclipse activity.

Transiting Lunar Eclipse Opposite Natal Mercury. Under the influence of this opposition, one becomes aware of emotional considerations that color decision-making. If either the lunar eclipse or natal Mercury is heavily afflicted, overreaction that produces reasoning which is too dispassionate and cold or, at the other extreme, emotional emphasis that overrides common sense is likely. The signs involved in this aspect and natal potentials determine the direction of overreaction and the degree of its extremity. Here, balance between feelings and the intellect is important if confusion and/or conflict are to be avoided and eclipse potentials developed along positive lines.

TRANSITING LUNAR ECLIPSE ASPECTS TO NATAL VENUS

An aspect formed between a transiting lunar eclipse and natal Venus stirs affections and creates desire for emotionally fulfilling relationships. Easy aspects point out circumstances and relationships that contribute to emotional satisfaction. Afflictions describe emotional attitudes and romantic tendencies that hinder the capacity to relate to others on an intimate basis. Financial interests associated with affairs influenced by a lunar eclipse/natal Venus aspect bear upon emotional security or the lack of it.

Transiting Lunar Eclipse Conjunct Natal Venus. This conjunction brings out pleasing qualities in one's nature and gives rise to feelings of happiness and harmony. It fosters warmth, congeniality and a sense of emotional security. Because the individual derives inner satisfaction and pleasure through activities and relationships influenced by this aspect, he or she tends to reach out to these affairs and the people involved in them. If the conjunction is afflicted, especially if it occupies a water sign, one often reacts in an overly emotional manner that displays inappropriate sentimentality. In any case, the friendly relations one establishes under the influence of this aspect help promote both lunar and solar eclipse potentials during the effective period.

Transiting Lunar Eclipse Sextile Natal Venus. This sextile produces a harmonious climate, a setting in which cordial relationships flourish. It describes available opportunities and fortunate conditions that offer emotional satisfaction and/or financial prosperity in agreement with natal potentials. Other people involved in the affairs influenced by this aspect usually benefit the individual in some way. Positive development of lunar eclipse affairs supports progress in solar eclipse affairs.

Transiting Lunar Eclipse Square Natal Venus. This square is associated with hidden frustrations and emotional blocks that hinder affectional expression and the capacity to sustain intimate relationships. It also identifies incorrect attitudes about money and material possessions, pointing to the need to develop a balanced perspective between practical and sentimental aspects of life. It is important to the development of affairs influenced by the lunar eclipse and natal Venus, as well as those activated by the solar eclipse(s) in the sequence, that the individual confront and deal with obstacles, emotional and material, revealed by this square.

Transiting Lunar Eclipse Trine Natal Venus. This trine generates a pleasant rapport with persons involved in affairs it influences. One's associates grant favors more willingly and lend emotional support more freely. As a rule, efforts directed into affairs associated with this aspect are well-received and rewarding; related activities contribute to development of solar eclipse potentials. This trine suggests financial gains as well as emotional and affectional rewards.

Transiting Lunar Eclipse Quincunx Natal Venus. This aspect yields clues to causes of inadequate emotional expression and/or misplaced affections. It describes the inability to convey feelings of love in intimate situations. Often, the individual's emotional security depends upon financial stability. Natal potentials reveal whether adjustment should be directed toward improving innate emotional patterns or toward correcting negative financial attitudes relating to affairs influenced by this quincunx, or both. Until problems are sorted out and adjusted, interests associated with the lunar eclipse and natal Venus are of little help in successfully developing solar eclipse potentials.

Transiting Lunar Eclipse Opposite Natal Venus. This opposition indicates discordant relationships empty of emotional fulfillment; it arouses inner dissatisfaction. It creates awareness of the need to form satisfying attachments. It exposes, if only to the individual, areas in which one is emotionally vulnerable. It also calls attention to counterproductive financial activities and extravagant habits. In order to utilize eclipse energies to best advantage, one must strive to balance emotional, affectional and material needs. Overemphasis in any one area distracts progress in lunar eclipse/natal Venus affairs and fails to generate support for solar eclipse development.

TRANSITING LUNAR ECLIPSE ASPECTS TO NATAL MARS

An aspect involving a transiting lunar eclipse and natal Mars lends emotional sensitivity to the passion and energy characteristic of Mars. Resultant action reflects emotional motivation as well as physical drive. Easy aspects soften the abrasiveness of Mars and lend emotional force to Martian energies. Afflictions tend to generate anger, quarrels and disruptive emotional displays.

Transiting Lunar Eclipse Conjunct Natal Mars. This aspect strengthens Martian sense of purpose with emotional force. There is much energy and passion here which, if structured along productive lines, can lead to solid achievements in affairs influenced by the conjunction, achievements that support positive development of solar eclipse potentials. If the conjunction is afflicted or in a weak sign, related activity is unlikely to produce substantial results. In order that the energy and intensity generated by this aspect be utilized effectively, direction is necessary. Without it, emotional excesses, anger and hostility drain physical drive and deplete emotional/instinctual resources.

Transiting Lunar Eclipse Sextile Natal Mars. This aspect harmonizes the physical and emotional natures so that one's inner resources support physical action. Lunar eclipse influence here is to refine the harsher qualities symbolic of Mars without compromising Martian initiative and boldness. Gains made in areas influenced by the sextile open opportunities through which solar eclipse potentials can be positively expressed and more fully developed.

Transiting Lunar Eclipse Square Natal Mars. This square describes emotional blocks that frustrate Martian energy and activity. It generates animosity and discord in the affairs it influences. It is important to success in these affairs and to full development of solar eclipse potentials that the individual not only curb impulsiveness and temperamental outbursts but also channel emotional and physical energies into constructive outlets.

Transiting Lunar Eclipse Trine Natal Mars. This trine generates harmony between emotional and physical drives. One is sensitive to and responsive to physical needs described by natal Mars. Personal action directed into affairs influenced by this aspect is supported by the inner self. Because one feels good inside about Martian activities, he or she develops confidence in handling these affairs, confidence that promotes fruitful action in activities directly influenced by the solar eclipse(s) in the sequence.

Transiting Lunar Eclipse Quincunx Natal Mars. This aspect points out the need to alter negative emotional traits and instinctive attitudes that slow progress in affairs influenced by the lunar eclipse and natal Mars. Energies must be directed toward positive emotional expression as well as constructive physical action. The key to utilizing affairs energized by this quincunx to reinforce solar eclipse potentials is in unifying emotional and physical drives to produce endeavors in which the individual feels emotionally secure.

Transiting Lunar Eclipse Opposite Natal Mars. This aspect, an especially discordant one, signals the need for emotional control and patience. Too often, the desire for emotional satisfaction prompts rash actions that compound problems and give rise to troublesome situations. If other factors in the horoscope confirm, tendencies toward combativeness and/or violence frequently manifest during the period of eclipse influence. The tension produced by this opposition creates awareness of attendant conflicts and the desire to do something about them. It is important that one take constructive action. A positive approach enables one to successfully meet the challenges presented in affairs influenced by the lunar eclipse and natal Mars and to advance these interests so they can fulfill their supportive role in solar eclipse activity. A negative response results in a flurry of fruitless endeavors accompanied by emotional disturbances.

TRANSITING LUNAR ECLIPSE ASPECTS TO NATAL JUPITER

A transiting lunar eclipse injects emotional and instinctual sentiments into ethical and religious attitudes when it aspects natal Jupiter. It stirs interest in abstract ideas, foreign cultures and travel. Frequently, during the period of eclipse activity, personal beliefs, convictions and philosophy undergo fundamental changes as one becomes more responsive to these facets of affairs influenced by the lunar eclipse and natal Jupiter.

Transiting Lunar Eclipse Conjunct Natal Jupiter. The good will and benevolence generated by this conjunction smooth the course of affairs it influences. It heralds a buoyant period that reflects hope, optimism and success. Events of the period help shape one's ethical and moral attitudes, attitudes that spill over into affairs activated by the solar eclipse(s) in the sequence. An afflicted conjunction warns the individual against groundless optimism and foolish generosity that prompt ill-advised ventures; too, misplaced sympathies can leave the individual vulnerable to exploitation.

Transiting Lunar Eclipse Sextile Natal Jupiter. High spirits and a prevailing sense of well-being accompany this sextile. It produces a climate that encourages generosity and gratitude. The affairs influenced by the lunar eclipse and natal Jupiter provide fertile opportunities for successful activities that can be utilized to promote development of solar eclipse potentials. These affairs represent promising avenues through which energies generated by lunar eclipse afflictions can be redirected toward gainful ends.

Transiting Lunar Eclipse Square Natal Jupiter. Because this aspect promotes emotional excesses and impractical views that impede progress in the affairs influenced by the lunar eclipse and natal Jupiter, it calls for emotional restraint and sound judgment. Only by clearing away obstacles described by this square can one advance the interests with which it is associated and utilize them to support solar eclipse activity. Often, events of the period during which the eclipse sequence is effective test one's integrity, moral standards and sense of propriety.

Transiting Lunar Eclipse Trine Natal Jupiter. This trine creates conditions that nurture hope, good will and emotional well-being. Usually, the affairs influenced by the lunar eclipse and natal Jupiter proceed smoothly. Energies produced by afflictions to the lunar eclipse or to natal Jupiter can be constructively channeled through these affairs. These interests also offer avenues for expansion of solar eclipse activity.

Transiting Lunar Eclipse Quincunx Natal Jupiter. This aspect clearly points to inherited habit patterns and negative emotional attitudes that color one's beliefs and ethical standards. It indicates misplaced sympathy, lack of moral integrity, insincerity and/or mawkish sentimentality as root causes of failings in affairs influenced by the lunar eclipse and natal Jupiter. One must look to the inner self for guidance in identifying and correcting defeating persuasions that produce philosophical and emotional immaturity. Once one confronts lacks shown by this quincunx and makes positive adjustments, attendant affairs develop more fully and can be utilized to assist the evolvement of solar eclipse potentials.

Transiting Lunar Eclipse Opposite Natal Jupiter. This opposition triggers awareness of inner conflicts that produce emotional discontent and challenge one's ethical standards and religious principles. Frequently, emotional considerations motivate changes in affairs influenced by this aspect when a successful outcome depends upon a logical approach. Overexpansion represents a threat to progress in these affairs as well as in those directly influenced by the solar eclipse(s) in the sequence. Advancement depends largely upon one's capacity to maintain proper perspective regarding interests energized by the lunar eclipse and governed by natal Jupiter.

TRANSITING LUNAR ECLIPSE ASPECTS TO NATAL SATURN

An aspect between a transiting lunar eclipse and natal Saturn encourages emotional stability and discipline to the degree described by the signs involved and natal potentials. Hard lunar eclipse/natal Saturn aspects frustrate emotional expression and often produce depression, whereas easy aspects curb emotional extremes and lend to emotional security. These aspects, easy or hard, encourage realism and emotional control, but insensitivity is not inspired, not even by hard aspects, unless the potential is contained in the natal horoscope.

Transiting Lunar Eclipse Conjunct Natal Saturn. This conjunction fosters emotional restraint and inner composure. It is especially helpful in a horoscope that projects extreme sensitivity of feelings and lack of emotional balance, for it lends to emotional control and inner poise. However, it also brings out tendencies toward self-pity, inner insecurity and moodiness if the natal horoscope portrays such inclinations. This aspect signals the necessity of a responsible approach to affairs it influences and also encourages realistic expectations. In order that affairs influenced by the lunar eclipse and natal Saturn progress to the point that they can assist solar eclipse potentials, it is important that one develop those interests along practical and conservative lines.

Transiting Lunar Eclipse Sextile Natal Saturn. The climate generated by this sextile promotes inner security, a sense of responsibility and emotional reserve. It produces ambitious opportunities that offer lasting results. The period during which this aspect is effective, usually one of steady progress unmarked by extreme highs and lows, demands conservative action if the affairs it influences are to proceed along positive lines and provide constructive support for development of solar eclipse potentials.

Transiting Lunar Eclipse Square Natal Saturn. The period during which this aspect is effective can be emotionally devastating. One senses lack of sympathy and understanding from associates involved in affairs influenced by this square and frequently reacts by stifling his or her own inner feelings. Failure to promote interests associated with the lunar eclipse and natal Saturn because of inner inhibitions or a gloomy outlook results in lack of progress which, in turn, leads to despondency, melancholy and discouragement. It is important that the individual overcome any sense of inferiority and take prudent action to keep affairs influenced by this aspect moving ahead, if but slowly, and to utilize them to support solar eclipse potentials.

Transiting Lunar Eclipse Trine Natal Saturn. The atmosphere created by this trine encourages emotional discipline and nurtures practical instincts. It helps clear away unrealistic attitudes that not only hinder development of affairs influenced by the lunar eclipse and natal Saturn but also stand in the way of solar eclipse potentials. Too, this aspect identifies constructive outlets for energies created by afflictions to the lunar eclipse and natal Saturn.

Transiting Lunar Eclipse Quincunx Natal Saturn. This quincunx points out areas in which failure to meet responsibilities and/or lack of emotional discipline limit success and create ill will. The individual may harbor an instinctive aversion to affairs influenced by the lunar eclipse and natal Saturn and thus fail to direct proper attention to them. However, in order to master inner uneasiness and develop responsible emotional attitudes, one must take positive steps to develop potentials of these interests. Progress in affairs activated by this aspect reinforces development of solar eclipse potentials.

Transiting Lunar Eclipse Opposite Natal Saturn. This opposition restricts emotional warmth and creates an inner sense of loneliness. Frequently, the individual feels that his or her efforts in areas influenced by this aspect are unappreciated and unrewarding and, therefore, he or she remains indifferent to these interests and aloof to persons involved in them. If one can harness the emotional tension generated by this aspect and direct it into constructive output that produces positive action in affairs energized by the lunar eclipse and natal Saturn, steady progress can be achieved in these areas as well as those influenced by the solar eclipse(s) belonging to the same sequence.

TRANSITING LUNAR ECLIPSE ASPECTS TO NATAL URANUS

An aspect formed by a transiting lunar eclipse and natal Uranus adds refreshing emotional overtones to the horoscope. It stimulates intuitive sensitivity and arouses altruistic instincts. Easy aspects bring out innovative qualities characteristic of Uranus; hard aspects stress the radical. A certain amount of unpredictability prevails while a lunar eclipse/natal Uranus aspect operates. As with any Uranian aspect, the only certainty lies in the promise for change. A positive response brings about progress and constructive changes. A negative reaction, usually accompanied by erratic emotional impulses and/or bizarre motivational instincts, reflects inability to cope with vicissitudes that beset affairs influenced by the lunar eclipse and natal Uranus.

Transiting Lunar Eclipse Conjunct Natal Uranus. This aspect signals emotional awakening. While it is in force, the individual experiences feelings and sensations to which he or she is unaccustomed. Because this aspect alerts one to previously unrecognized facets of situations and relationships it influences, one usually acquires progressive attitudes that advance these interests and support development of solar eclipse potentials. Afflictions to this conjunction provoke capricious emotional urges which prompt precipitous actions. The individual who is not caught off guard by rash impulses, one who copes with the fast pace of events and abrupt changes that accompany this aspect, enjoys a promising period that generates anticipation and produces progress.

Transiting Lunar Eclipse Sextile Natal Uranus. This sextile heralds unprecedented opportunities which reveal exciting avenues of activity. The atmosphere surrounding affairs it influences produces an emotional lift that prompts one to reach out to new friends and experiences, to develop novel interests and to experiment with innovative techniques. Advances made in areas activated by the lunar eclipse and Uranus encourage progressive endeavors in affairs directly influenced by the solar eclipse(s) in the sequence.

Transiting Lunar Eclipse Square Natal Uranus. This square describes obstacles created by emotional caprice and radical actions. It activates idiosyncrasies contained in the natal horoscope and generates emotional instability to a degree consistent with natal potentials. The period during which this aspect is effective can be a trying time. Most individuals feel pulled in too many directions at once; many suffer from great emotional stress and anxiety, and some are subject to emotional aberrations. Usually, one experiences a sense of urgency that prompts frenetic activity. A positive response to this aspect brings out ingenuity and lends to innovation. Nevertheless, the energy generated by this square needs firm direction in order to produce advancement in affairs it influences and those activated by the solar eclipse(s) in the sequence. Without direction, accelerated activity results in pointless changes and abortive efforts.

Transiting Lunar Eclipse Trine Natal Uranus. Futuristic conditions generated by this trine promote innovative techniques and progressive changes. The individual experiences a sense of expectancy that stimulates the emotions and attracts him or her to new interests and different people. Unusual circumstances foster advancement in affairs influenced by the lunar eclipse and natal Uranus and open avenues through which to extend activity of the solar eclipse(s) in the sequence. Astounding psychic revelations often accompany this aspect.

Transiting Lunar Eclipse Quincunx Natal Uranus. This quincunx identifies inconsistent emotional attitudes and irresponsible actions as causes of instability and failure in affairs and relationships it influences. In order that the period during which this aspect is effective be productive of progress, the individual must change negative attitudes and reform ineffectual practices. Successful advances in lunar eclipse/natal Uranus affairs (which in turn contribute to solar eclipse development) depend upon the capacity to develop unwavering emotional force that supports sustained efforts.

Transiting Lunar Eclipse Opposite Natal Uranus. The emotional tension generated by this opposition stimulates the compulsion to be free of confining relationships; it fosters almost total disregard for consequences of ill-considered actions. Sudden rifts, separations, estrangements and atypical behavior often accompany this aspect. If affairs influenced by this aspect are to be advanced along positive lines and utilized to reinforce development of solar eclipse potentials, it is imperative that the individual exercise as much control as possible over changes that take place during the period of eclipse influence, that he or she curb impulses which are normally uncharacteristic, act responsibly and avoid intentionally disrupting matters.

TRANSITING LUNAR ECLIPSE ASPECTS TO NATAL NEPTUNE

An aspect from a transiting lunar eclipse to natal Neptune engenders empathy and receptivity. One grows more attuned to vibrations that emanate from other people and to psychic influences that permeate the atmosphere during the eclipse effective period. Easy aspects inspire vision and imagination. Hard aspects contribute to emotional withdrawal and escapism.

Transiting Lunar Eclipse Conjunct Natal Neptune. This aspect stimulates the subconscious bringing to the fore imaginative and psychic inclinations. It stirs tendencies to daydream and fantasize. It also opens the door to mystical and spiritual experiences; it sheds light on past lives and karmic responsibilities. If the conjunction is afflicted, negative Neptunian qualities may emerge. Hallucinations, drug or alcohol abuse and/or emotional withdrawal are possible if potentials are shown in the natal horoscope. It is important that the individual maintain a realistic point of view about affairs and relationships influenced by this aspect and not succumb to false illusions. Unfortunately, fallacies associated with lunar eclipse/natal Neptune interests color development of solar eclipse potentials.

Transiting Lunar Eclipse Sextile Natal Neptune. This sextile, inspirational in nature, generates opportunities that encourage one to draw upon inner and spiritual resources. It attracts psychic vibrations of the highest order and contributes to the evolvement of clairvoyant tendencies or other Neptunian psychic abilities shown in the natal horoscope. Progress of affairs influenced by this aspect and utilization of these interests to reinforce solar eclipse objectives depends in part upon the stage of inner development one realizes during the period of eclipse effectiveness.

Transiting Lunar Eclipse Square Natal Neptune. This square reveals hidden psychological motives and groundless fears which block progress in affairs influenced by the lunar eclipse and natal Neptune. It calls attention to emotional disturbances and spiritual misconceptions that hinder development. In order to advance interests associated with this aspect and utilize them in support of solar eclipse potentials, it is important that the individual develop emotional and spiritual attitudes which are both positive and realistic and also correct specious habits and negative escapist tendencies.

Transiting Lunar Eclipse Trine Natal Neptune. This aspect, associated with the inner nature, describes circumstances and avenues that foster mystic experiences, psychic happenings and spiritual growth. It enhances natural sensitivity and impressionability depicted in the natal horoscope. It also encourages one to cultivate dormant mediumistic or clairvoyant aptitudes. Inner growth achieved through activities influenced by this trine assists one's efforts in affairs energized by the solar eclipse(s) in the sequence.

Transiting Lunar Eclipse Quincunx Natal Neptune. This aspect points to emotional delusions. Because the individual is unsure how he or she feels about affairs and relationships influenced by the lunar eclipse and natal Neptune, related efforts are haphazard and largely ineffectual. Lack of success creates a sense of futility that can cause one to withdraw from these interests. However, this quincunx signals the need to examine one's feelings and inner attitudes, to probe for the blind spot within himself/herself that masks reality in order to clear the inner confusions experienced and cope with the actualities of attendant situations. Once muddled affairs associated with this aspect are straightened out, they can be utilized to constructively support solar eclipse activity.

Transiting Lunar Eclipse Opposite Natal Neptune. This opposition stirs interest in the intangibles of life. It creates awareness of spiritual and emotional needs and sharpens one's natural subconscious instincts and psychic abilities. But it also produces hypersensitivity that enhances one's vulnerability to negative psychic forces. It warns against deceptive spiritual practices and cultism. It is important to inner growth that the individual not follow false spiritual paths or become involved in the black arts. The spiritual development, sentiment and intuitivity that come under this aspect when its energies are properly directed enable one to relate to affairs influenced by the lunar eclipse and natal Neptune as well as those energized by the solar eclipse(s) in the sequence.

TRANSITING LUNAR ECLIPSE ASPECTS TO NATAL PLUTO

A lunar eclipse that aspects natal Pluto energizes inner forces associated with that planet and sharpens one's sensitivity to and awareness of the subconscious and its functions. Intense emotions manifest during the period of eclipse influence, emotions some people find difficult to handle. Others who find positive outlets for the powerful emotional energy generated by a lunar eclipse/natal Pluto aspect acquire inner strength and sense of purpose which enables them to deal with the unknown as well as the familiar. Easy aspects signify the means through which lunar eclipse/natal Pluto energies can be channeled productively with minimal emotional distress. Emotional coercion and violent emotional outbursts are associated with hard aspects.

Transiting Lunar Eclipse Conjunct Natal Pluto. This aspect evokes strong passions; one experiences profound feelings of love, hate, joy, sorrow, etc. Reaction depends largely upon natal potentials and the current emotional state. Nervous individuals tend to become extremely excitable, and many find it difficult to channel these energies constructively. Those who exercise excessive emotional restraint suffer from internal emotional complexities which they neither understand nor have the capacity to release in an acceptable manner; frequently, these people build up to an emotional explosion. This aspect is especially helpful to actors/actresses and others who utilize vivid emotional expression, for it increases one's natural ability to experience and express emotions. Positive direction of aspect energy lends sustaining force to efforts connected with solar eclipse activity as well as to those directly influenced by the conjunction.

Transiting Lunar Eclipse Sextile Natal Pluto. This sextile generates emotional strength; it identifies avenues and relationships that provide emotional support and strengthen inner purpose. It also enhances powers of recall, enables one to utilize subconscious perceptions, nurtures spiritual growth and fosters intuitive development. The positive emotional expression and control of negative feelings associated with this aspect contribute to advancement of affairs influenced by the lunar eclipse and natal Pluto; these advancements, in turn, lend strong support to solar eclipse activity.

Transiting Lunar Eclipse Square Natal Pluto. This square describes inner frustrations, subconscious blocks and/or coercive tendencies that impede positive emotional expression and create spiritual reservations. The individual may exhibit powerful emotional force that others sense as threatening, or, conversely, he or she may feel emotionally menaced by prevailing circumstances and relationships influenced by the lunar eclipse and Pluto. Positive utilization of aspect energy enables one to overcome the obstacles this square represents and also contributes to development of solar eclipse potentials.

Transiting Lunar Eclipse Trine Natal Pluto. This aspect produces circumstances that help one get rid of emotional blocks and undesirable instincts. It enables one to capitalize upon emotional strengths and positive subconcious attitudes. The magnetic emotional appeal that usually accompanies this trine attracts people who, in some way, benefit the individual and his or her interests. Fortunate situations develop which promote affairs influenced by the lunar eclipse, natal Pluto and, perhaps indirectly, those of the solar eclipse(s) in the sequence.

Transiting Lunar Eclipse Quincunx Natal Pluto. This quincunx identifies areas in which one tends to abuse emotional powers. It brings into play an overwhelming sense of inner power that prods one to dominate others through emotional control. The key to progress in affairs influenced by the lunar eclipse and natal Pluto and their contribution to advancement of solar eclipse potentials lies with positive emotional development. This aspect also deals with spiritual evolution and other esoteric matters associated with Pluto.

Transiting Lunar Eclipse Opposite Natal Pluto. This opposition brings out subconscious tendencies to control situations and people through emotional coercion. In a highly afflicted horoscope, one may resort to cruelty and abuse as means of obtaining emotional satisfaction. In order that one not be victimized by his or her own emotions, it is important to direct the powerful emotional energy produced by this aspect into constructive outlets. Failure to do so results in a decadent and ofttimes violent state of affairs that precludes constructive development of interests associated with the lunar eclipse and natal Pluto and contributes nothing to solar eclipse objectives.

TRANSITING LUNAR ASPECTS TO NATAL MOON'S NODES

Aspects between a transiting lunar eclipse and the natal Moon's Nodes call attention to potentials for emotional experiences as described at the North Node and potentials associated with inborn patterns symbolized by the South Node. Both easy and hard aspects relate affairs of the house occupied by the lunar eclipse to the unfolding of the promise of the Nodes in accordance with the natures of the aspects and natal potentials.

Transiting Lunar Eclipse Conjunct Natal North Node Opposite Natal South Node. These aspects heighten one's awareness of the subconscious and sharpen one's natural instincts. Unless the Nodes are heavily afflicted, the period of eclipse influence is an advantageous one during which one instinctively reaches out emotionally to people and affairs associated with the transiting lunar eclipse and natal North Node. The lunar eclipse/natal South Node opposition alerts one to limitations imposed at the natal South Node, and the individual is motivated emotionally to do something about them. Situations that evolve around the lunar eclipse/natal North Node conjunction contribute to the resolution of South Node problems.

Transiting Lunar Eclipse Conjunct Natal South Node Opposite Natal North Node. This aspect arrangement emphasizes the need to utilize inner energies constructively, the need to confront negative habit patterns depicted by the natal South Node and turn them around before one can reach out to positive natal North Node experiences. Often, the individual feels uncomfortable with affairs of the house occupied by the natal North Node, at least during the period of eclipse activity, and, because of emotional inhibitions, fails to respond to these interests. The best approach to affairs of the activated houses, opposite each other in the horoscope, is one that maintains proper balance between polar interests.

Transiting Lunar Eclipse Sextile Natal North Node Trine Natal South Node. Opportune circumstances that stem from affairs of the houses occupied by the lunar eclipse and the natal North Node foster positive emotional experiences that not only contribute to inner satisfaction and emotional growth but also open up avenues through which one can overcome subconscious blocks which impede growth described at the natal South Node. Lunar energies and the interests of the house it occupies can be readily utilized in developing the natal promise of both Nodes.

Transiting Lunar Eclipse Sextile Natal South Node Trine Natal North Node. During the period that these aspects operate, one feels at ease with relationships and circumstances influenced by the lunar eclipse and natal Nodes. Feeling emotionally secure, one relates comfortably to experiential natal North Node interests; being sensitive to natal South Node inklings, one is able to redirect negative attitudes. These aspects encourage positive emotional expression and contribute to inner fulfillment.

Transiting Lunar Eclipse Square Natal North Node Square Natal South Node. The period during which this T-square is in effect can be an emotionally frustrating one for the individual who fails to utilize lunar eclipse energies constructively. The lunar eclipse, occupying the focal point of the T-square, identifies affairs and relationships through which emotional growth can be achieved, growth that supports potentials of both Nodes. It also points out inner biases and/or negative emotional characteristics that, if left unchecked, hinder emotional development and block the promise of the Nodes. Affairs of the house occupied by the lunar eclipse demand proper attention if progress is to be achieved and emotional satisfaction gained.

Transiting Lunar Eclipse Square Natal South Node Square Natal North Node. See *"Transiting Lunar Eclipse Square Natal North Node Square Natal South Node."*

Transiting Lunar Eclipse Trine Natal North Node Sextile Natal South Node. See *"Transiting Lunar Eclipse Sextile Natal South Node Trine Natal North Node."*

Transiting Lunar Eclipse Trine Natal South Node Sextile Natal North Node. See *"Transiting Lunar Eclipse Sextile Natal North Node Trine Natal South Node."*

Transiting Lunar Eclipse Quincunx Natal North Node Semi-sextile Natal South Node. This configuration suggests that failure to benefit from natal North Node experiences and overcome natal South Node limitations is rooted in unacceptable emotional expression and inner prejudices. It signals a need to redirect inner energies along positive lines. Adjustment of attitudes regarding affairs influenced by the lunar eclipse and natal North Node must come before the promise of the natal North Node can develop and lunar energies can be utilized to assist natal South Node potentials.

Transiting Lunar Eclipse Quincunx Natal South Node Semi-sextile Natal North Node. These aspects indicate that although the individual feels comfortable with natal North Node interests, he or she is insensitive to people and affairs represented by the house occupied by the lunar eclipse. This lack of emotional rapport restrains one from reaching out to natal North Node experiences and hinders the capacity to deal with detrimental patterns symbolic of the natal South Node. Emotional adjustments effected through lunar relationships and interests clear the way for positive expression at the natal North Node and enable one to overcome negative natal South Node potentials.

Transiting Lunar Eclipse Opposite Natal North Node Conjunct Natal South Node. See *"Transiting Lunar Eclipse Conjunct Natal South Node Opposite Natal North Node."*

Transiting Lunar Eclipse Opposite Natal South Node Conjunct Natal North Node. See *"Transiting Lunar Eclipse Conjunct Natal North Node Opposite Natal South Node."*

TRANSITING LUNAR ECLIPSE ASPECTS TO THE NATAL ASCENDANT AND NATAL DESCENDANT

An aspect from a transiting lunar eclipse to the natal Ascendant describes the emotional expression one projects during the period of eclipse influence. Its complementary aspect to the natal Descendant reflects the emotional rapport that colors seventh house relationships at the time.

Transiting Lunar Eclipse Conjunct Natal Ascendant Opposite Natal Descendant. Unless the lunar eclipse appears in the sign following or preceding that occupied by the Ascendant as infrequently happens, these aspects directly link like emotional and personal qualities; traits associated with the Ascendant become more prominent during the period of eclipse influence. At the time, inner security and emotional confidence are of prime concern to the individual. One's emotional well-being or lack of it is reflected in seventh house attitudes and relationships. If the Ascendant is highly afflicted, emotional instability and/or disappointing relationships are possible. Ill health can be a factor, especially in a woman's horoscope, because of the emotional drain prevalent during the period.

Transiting Lunar Eclipse Conjunct Natal Descendant Opposite Natal Ascendant. These aspects emphasize the necessity of developing positive emotional attributes that will enable one to maintain compatible relationships. Other people who share one's life have much to do with shaping one's emotional attitudes during the period of eclipse influence. The individual usually seeks out people with whom he or she can relate on an emotional level. These aspects foster sensitivity and receptivity; some individuals, especially those who lack innate emotional strength, grow emotionally dependent upon their spouse, partners or other close associates.

Transiting Lunar Eclipse Sextile Natal Ascendant Trine Natal Descendant. These aspects generate emotionally satisfying conditions that enhance personal expression, enrich seventh house relationships and lend to a harmonious rapport with the public. They also produce opportunities which promote personal growth and emotional well-being. Energies created by afflictions to the lunar eclipse can be constructively channeled through first and seventh house avenues while these aspects operate.

Transiting Lunar Eclipse Sextile Natal Descendant Trine Natal Ascendant. These aspects promote an easy flow of emotional expression. The individual projects emotional appeal and a pleasing image that attracts beneficial people and fortunate situations. Because one is sensitive to the feelings of others, he or she instinctively senses the right thing to say or do to further first and seventh house interests. During the period of eclipse activity, opportunities relating to marriage or partnership frequently arise.

Transiting Lunar Eclipse Square Natal Ascendant Square Natal Descendant. This configuration indicates emotional contradictions that disturb the personality and create discord in seventh house affairs and relationships. It is through affairs of the house occupied by the lunar eclipse, placed at the focal point of a T-square completed by the horizontal angles, that the individual must begin to resolve emotional conflicts, for upheavals in this area reflect adversely upon first and seventh house interests. As lunar eclipse energies gain positive direction in the lunar house, they contribute to progress in other matters influenced by these aspects. Obstacles represented by these squares are of the sort that inhibit personal expression and impede marital and partnership activities.

Transiting Lunar Eclipse Square Natal Descendent Square Natal Ascendant. See *"Transiting Lunar Eclipse Square Natal Ascendant Square Natal Descendant."*

Transiting Lunar Eclipse Trine Natal Ascendant Sextile Natal Descendant. See *"Transiting Lunar Eclipse Sextile Natal Descendant Trine Natal Ascendant."*

Transiting Lunar Eclipse Trine Natal Descendant Sextile Natal Ascendant. See *"Transiting Lunar Eclipse Sextile Natal Ascendant Trine Natal Descendant."*

Transiting Lunar Eclipse Quincunx Natal Ascendant Semi-sextile Natal Descendant. This aspect arrangement suggests that lack of sensitivity to affairs energized by the lunar eclipse impedes progress in that area and that emotional problems detract from personal expression. In order to reach full potentials, one needs to correct emotional deficiencies and to adjust his or her approach to lunar affairs. Usually, the cooperation of spouse, partners or other close associates is available; their assistance can help the individual make adjustments essential to development of lunar interests, personal growth and inner satisfaction.

Transiting Lunar Eclipse Quincunx Natal Descendant Semi-Sextile Natal Ascendant. These aspects indicate the need to reach out emotionally to others in order to sustain fulfilling relationships. One usually tends to blame unhappy situations and unproductive associations on other persons involved. This negative attitude makes adjustment especially difficult in marriage and other intimate relationships. These aspects show that the individual is responsive to his or her own emotions, but must learn to be sensitive to the feelings and needs of others.

Transiting Lunar Eclipse Opposite Natal Ascendant Conjunct Natal Descendant. See *"Transiting Lunar Eclipse Conjunct Natal Descendant Opposite Natal Ascendant."*

Transiting Lunar Eclipse Opposite Natal Descendant Conjunct Natal Ascendant. See *"Transiting Lunar Eclipse Conjunct Natal Ascendant Opposite Natal Descendant.*

TRANSITING LUNAR ECLIPSE ASPECTS TO THE NATAL MIDHEAVEN AND NATAL IMUM COELI (NADIR)

An aspect formed by a transiting lunar eclipse to the natal MC (Midheaven) and its complementary aspect to the natal IC (Imum Coeli) bring into play feelings and instincts associated with worldly ambitions, public achievements, family interests and home life.

Transiting Lunar Eclipse Conjunct Natal MC Opposite Natal IC. These aspects bring the career into prominence during the period of eclipse influence. The period often produces change in professional status. The individual, sensitive to shifts and variations that affect tenth house interests, is able to make advantageous moves in keeping with prevailing circumstances. If the lunar eclipse/MC conjunction is afflicted, one must work around potential adversities in order to avoid possible setbacks. Generally, one derives greater inner satisfaction from professional interests and business associations than from family relationships and home life while these aspects are in effect.

Transiting Lunar Eclipse Conjunct Natal IC Opposite Natal MC. This aspect configuration stresses fourth house interests. One tends to lean heavily upon the home situation and family relationships for emotional reassurance. Quite frequently, the individual effects changes that alter the family lifestyle or the living quarters. Extensive home improvements or a move to a different residence often take place while these aspects are in effect. Increased family interaction and greater interest in the home are characteristic of the period. These aspects also stir psychic abilities and interest in the occult.

Transiting Lunar Eclipse Sextile Natal MC Trine Natal IC. These aspects give rise to career opportunities that usually stem from affairs or associations involving the house occupied by the lunar eclipse. They enhance one's capacity to maintain a friendly rapport with persons who influence professional interests. Usually, harmonious domestic conditions that add to one's inner sense of well-being prevail during the period of eclipse influence. Family support contributes much to career advancement.

Transiting Lunar Eclipse Sextile Natal IC Trine Natal MC. These aspects generate a satisfying period during which the individual derives emotional security and inner contentment through fourth and tenth house activities and associations. Avenues influenced by the lunar eclipse provide opportunities that enhance the quality of home life and strengthen family relationships. Harmonious family interaction and smoothly flowing career/business endeavors are associated with these aspects.

Transiting Lunar Eclipse Square Natal MC Square Natal IC. This aspect arrangement suggests that the inability to relate to people on an emotional level blocks career advancement and creates family discord. Frustrating experiences encountered in the profession and at home cause emotional insecurities that inhibit progressive action in affairs of the house occupied by the lunar eclipse. With the lunar eclipse at the focal point of a T-square involving the vertical angles, it is important that one stabilize lunar affairs and direct tenth and fourth house interests along positive lines.

Transiting Lunar Eclipse Square Natal IC Square Natal MC. See *"Transiting Lunar Eclipse Square Natal MC Square Natal IC."*

Transiting Lunar Eclipse Trine Natal MC Sextile Natal IC. See *"Transiting Lunar Eclipse Sextile Natal IC Trine Natal MC."*

Transiting Lunar Eclipse Trine Natal IC Sextile Natal MC. See *"Transiting Lunar Eclipse Sextile Natal MC Trine Natal IC."*

Transiting Lunar Eclipse Quincunx Natal MC Semi-sextile Natal IC. These aspects signal the need to rethink worldly goals, to redirect career endeavors and/or to strive to attain a more comfortable emotional rapport with professional associates. It is up to the individual to adjust attitudes or actions that interfere with full development of tenth house potentials. Examination of the lunar eclipse and the affairs it influences will give clues as to the nature and direction of necessary adjustments. Usually, home-related interests offer some release for emotional frustrations, and family relationships provide emotional support and contribute to inner well-being during the period these aspects are in effect.

Transiting Lunar Eclipse Quincunx Natal IC Semi-sextile Natal MC. These aspects indicate that the individual is insensitive to home interests and emotionally inhibited with family members. Lack of emotional warmth creates stilted family interaction. One feels freer to express emotions on the impersonal basis associated with the career climate than on the more intimate level of the family. The individual needs to overcome inner restraint and outwardly express feelings. Too, an adjustment in attitude toward affairs of the house occupied by the lunar eclipse can help improve matters in all areas influenced by these aspects.

Transiting Lunar Eclipse Opposite Natal MC Conjunct Natal IC. See *"Transiting Lunar Eclipse Conjunct Natal IC Opposite Natal MC."*

Transiting Lunar Eclipse Opposite Natal IC Conjunct Natal MC. See *"Transiting Lunar Eclipse Conjunct Natal MC Opposite Natal IC."*

TRANSITING LUNAR ECLIPSE ASPECTS TO PROGRESSED PLANETS AND ANGLES

The procedure for adapting interpretations of aspects between a transiting lunar eclipse and natal planets or angles to those involving progressed planets or angles is the same as that described in the section entitled "Transiting Solar Eclipse Aspects to Progressed Planets and Angles" in Chapter 5. Bear in mind that although orbs remain the same for eclipse aspects involving progressed points as for natal, only *exact* (1 degree orb) eclipse/progressed planet-angle aspects carry the same weight as their natal counterparts unless accompanying astrological factors as noted in Chapter 5 reinforce an inexact aspect to give it added strength in the horoscope.

CHAPTER 7

DELINEATION TECHNIQUES

Many factors enter into eclipse delineation, some seemingly insignificant. However, none can be arbitrarily omitted from analysis. Each must be considered and weighed in light of all other contributing factors. The following guidelines summarize procedures discussed in Chapters 1-6 and introduce additional interpretational material not found elsewhere in this book.

1. ASTROLOGICAL FRAME OF REFERENCE. In order to assess an individual's reaction to eclipse stimuli and evaluate the emphasis that an eclipse sequence exerts in a particular horoscope, the astrologer must examine the specific frame of reference within which eclipses of interest operate. The frame of reference described by natal and progressed potentials and transits that influence a horoscope during the eclipse period structures eclipse activity within that particular horoscope. Basic sign, house and aspect meanings must be adapted to relate to the individual's frame of reference and must fit within its structure. Study natal and progressed potentials and transits to get a clear picture of current astrological conditions applicable to the horoscope of interest and analyze eclipse factors accordingly. To be valid, eclipse findings must relate to horoscope potentials.

2. STRENGTH OF ECLIPSE ACTIVITY. Note the classification to which an eclipse belongs. Generally speaking, without considering other pertinent factors, the degree of activation an eclipse generates in a horoscope compares to the strength of perturbations it produces in cosmic energy fields. Therefore, it seems plausible that a total or annular solar eclipse induces stronger horoscope activation than does a partial solar eclipse and that a total lunar eclipse elicits stronger reaction than either a partial lunar eclipse or an appulse. However, other factors in a horoscope lend strength to eclipse activity, especially aspects. For example, a heavily aspected partial eclipse will have greater impact upon an individual than un unaspected total eclipse.

3. **ECLIPSE RETURNS.** Being cyclic in nature, many solar eclipses observe a regular nineteen-year Metonic return; others fail to do so. To be interpreted as a return, a solar eclipse must conjunct a prior eclipse within 2 degrees 30' of its orb. During a person's lifetime, the regularity of eclipse returns correlates to the rate of evolutionary development described by eclipse activity. An eclipse which recurs at regular nineteen-year Metonic intervals reflects a natural rhythmic pattern of evolution as natal potentials unfold. An irregular return indicates sporadic development. Progress quickens during a return period of less than nineteen years; growth slows during a long return interval and may even come to a halt if the individual fails to realize the necessity of developing eclipse associated potentials. In rare instances, an eclipse appears only once in a particular degree of the zodiac during a person's lifetime, observing no return. Such a singular eclipse, lacking developmental flow, may mark the onset of a stagnant period in which growth in the area energized by the eclipse comes to a standstill unless the individual recognizes and overcomes limitations inherent in the horoscope, or it may indicate a final phase of development during which the individual, having nearly attained perfection in a prior lifetime, is then reaching for the highest plateau of development in the area of horoscope activation. The horoscope contains clues as to which situation applies. If limiting factors are present, the individual must deal with them before natal potentials can be fully realized.

The position an eclipse holds in a series of returns indicates the stage of development associated with the time interval between that eclipse and the next one in the series. The first solar eclipse in a series of returns, associated with the initial stage of development, marks the beginning phase of growth in relation to the level described by natal potentials. The final return begins the period during which the individual can reach the highest potential shown in the horoscope. Intermediate returns in the series direct attention to related affairs and signal that it is time to move upward on the ladder of development. If one has not progressed during the prior stage, demands are twofold, for one developmental step is built upon the prior one. For example, assume an eclipse, the first of a series of returns, activates the first house of a horoscope. Personal development is at stake. If self-awareness is not shown in the horoscope, the individual must strive for self-identity and self-understanding, for one cannot develop potentials that go unrecognized. When the first return occurs, the individual, having achieved self-recognition, should be ready to reach out to developmental experiences. If he or she failed to progress during the initial period, then the second stage is delayed until the first is completed, or both stages progress concurrently.

4. **POLAR SETS.** When interpreting a polar set (Refer to Chapter 3), analyze the flow of activity that links each constituent eclipse. Each member eclipse, other than the first which introduces the fundamentals of the set, must be analyzed according to the emphasis of preceding eclipses belonging to that polar set. Too, note whether or not prior like polar sets have energized the horoscope. A first-time polar set experience introduces basic concepts; later like polar sets build upon these concepts, with each succeeding set increasing the growth potential in the areas of interest. For example, a first-time first/seventh or seventh/first house polar set usually occurs during childhood. A youngster's individualistic tendencies take shape as budding concepts of "self" (as opposed to the image projected by parents and/or siblings) begins to develop. A close friend or school chum fulfills the role of seventh house counterpart. When the same set recurs in adult years, that person turns to a marriage or business partner to fulfill seventh house needs.

5. **ECLIPSE DISPOSITOR.** Consider the planet in a horoscope that disposits an eclipse of interest. The dispositor brings into play qualities not necessarily directly associated with the eclipse and emphasizes others that are.

A well-aspected dispositor brings out positive characteristics associated with the sign occupied by the eclipse; an afflicted dispositor lends to negative sign expression. Eclipse sign expression also reflects subtle traits symbolic of the sign its dispositor occupies. For example, sign expression of an eclipse whose dispositor is in Cancer reflects some of the sensitivity attributed to that sign. A dispositor in Leo adds flamboyant touches to eclipse sign expression; one in Sagittarius injects enthusiasm.

If no astrological factors other than dispositorship link an eclipse with its dispositor, the dispositor's influence in eclipse activity is comparatively weak unless the dispositor is very strong and well-placed in the horoscope. A mutual reception, aspect or other astrological tie between an eclipse and its dispositor increases the dispositor's influence on the eclipse.

6. SIGN INTERPRETATION. Weigh the influence of the eclipse dispositor, the decan sub-ruler, duad sub-ruler and, in the case of a solar eclipse, the initial eclipse of the Saros series to which it belongs. Consider the zodiacal relationship (opposite or quincunx by sign) that exists between solar and lunar eclipses that occur in the same sequence. Note the emphasis that the sign an eclipse occupies exerts in the horoscope. A sign that is angular or heavily populated with planets emerges more strongly in eclipse activity than one which is intercepted or devoid of natal planets. For basic meanings of solar eclipses in the signs refer to Chapter 1; for lunar eclipse sign meanings refer to Chapter 2.

7. HOUSE INTERPRETATION. Note the house relationship (opposite or angle of distress) that exists between solar and lunar eclipses belonging to the same sequence. Examine the house the eclipse occupies and its affairs. Consider the sign on the cusp, its planetary ruler, the natural ruler of the house, the planets it houses, interception if such exists and aspects that influence the house. Orient interpretation to the natal and progressed potentials of the house. For basic meanings of solar eclipses in the houses refer to Chapter 3; for lunar eclipses in the houses refer to Chapter 4.

8. ECLIPSE LOCATION CHARTS. Erect an eclipse chart for the time of the appropriate new or full Moon at the location of the residence of the person whose chart you are examining or for the site of an event in which you are interested. Use natal orbs for aspects within the chart. An eclipse chart describes the general nature of event trends in the locality for which it is erected during the period of eclipse influence. The Ascendant and first house give a general description of the nature of event trends; the MC and tenth house describe their impact upon the public. The eclipse, the sign and house it occupies, and its aspects reveal more specific clues as to nature, impact and type of events possible. Study of third house factors (sign on the cusp, its ruler, planets it contains, Mercury, applicable aspects) yields clues to the eclipse message. A planet intercepted or retrograde in the third house masks the message, or at least parts of it. A malefic in the third house gives a warning signal as does a malefic conjunct an angle or chart ruler. An eclipse chart, which can apply to thousands of people, gives no specific information until it is compared with a horoscope of interest. Comparison of an eclipse chart with the horoscope of an individual (or event) gives added insight into eclipse influence in that horoscope.

9. ECLIPSE ASPECTS. Aspect the eclipse and, in the case of a solar eclipse, the initial eclipse of its Saros series. Use 5 degrees orb for major zodiacal eclipse aspects to natal and progressed planets or angles and 2 degrees for minor aspects. Narrow the orb to 1 degree for eclipse parallels, contraparallels and *all* initial eclipse aspects. Initial eclipse aspects operate through eclipse energies and are supportive in nature. They tie in affairs of the planets aspected with eclipse potentials. Exact hard initial eclipse aspects can manifest as eclipse-related events if other horoscope factors support event potentials.

When interpreting an eclipse aspect, consider the nature of the aspected planet and its influence in the horoscope. Study the interrelationships between the aspect of interest and other eclipse aspects. The tighter the orb of an aspect, the more influential it is within its limits. That is, an exact semi-sextile is not more influential than an inexact trine, but it is more influential than a wider semi-sextile. Refer to Chapter 5 for interpretations of solar eclipse aspects, to Chapter 6 for meanings of lunar eclipse aspects.

10. **THE UNASPECTED ECLIPSE.** An unaspected eclipse is not powerless. Its energy is there to be utilized, but it is more difficult to do so without direct channels, via aspects, for release of that energy. Eclipse energies can be funneled through its dispositor, a planet with which it is in mutual reception and, for a solar eclipse, through its initial eclipse. Before judging an eclipse "unaspected," check midpoints. An eclipse aspect to a midpoint (1 degree orb only) energizes potentials of both planets involved and channels eclipse energies accordingly.

11. **MANIFESTATION OF ECLIPSE-RELATED EVENTS.** A hard eclipse aspect to a planet or angle in a horoscope represents the astrological seed for an event, a seed that remains dormant until a progressed or transiting planet triggers awakening by forming an exact hard aspect with a related point. The most obvious triggering action occurs when the eclipse point is subsequently aspected. However, other exact hard progressed/transit aspects effectively trigger an eclipse potential to manifest an event. An exact hard aspect to the eclipse dispositor, to the midpoint of the eclipse and a planet it aspects and, if the eclipse occupies a midpoint, to either planet involved can trigger an eclipse-related event. In the case of a solar eclipse, a triggering aspect to its initial eclipse can activate the event potential shown by the eclipse. An exact hard aspect to a point in the appropriate eclipse location chart in combination with hard aspects to related natal and/or progressed points can also touch off an eclipse-related event. When a major eclipse-related event occurs, one usually finds several triggering aspects that operate simultaneously, one or more of which are partile or within minutes of partile.

Eclipse interpretation varies with the individual. No eclipse statement, no general interpretation applies exactly as is to any one person. Detailed examination of eclipse potentials in relationship to individual horoscopes reveals developmental patterns and event trends unique to each person.

APPENDIX

TWENTIETH CENTURY SOLAR AND LUNAR ECLIPSES

The following table of solar and lunar eclipses that appear in the twentieth century, from *Eclipses: Astrological Guideposts* by Rose Lineman (1984), is reproduced with permission of the publisher, American Federation of Astrologers, Inc., P.O. Box 22040, Tempe, Arizona 85282.

TABLE I - SOLAR AND LUNAR ECLIPSES
1900 - 1999

GMT DATE	SERIES	LONGITUDE	TYPE
05/28/00	10S	6°47' ♊	☉-T
06/13/00	10N	21°39' ♐	☽-A
11/22/00	11N	29°33' ♏	☉-A
12/06/00	11S	13°53' ♊	☽-A
05/03/01	11N	12°36' ♏	☽-A
05/18/01	11S	26°34' ♉	☉-T
10/27/01	12S	3°30' ♉	☽-P
11/11/01	12N	18°14' ♏	☉-A
04/08/02	12S-E*	17°48' ♈	☉-P
04/22/02	12N	1°42' ♏	☽-T
05/07/02	12S	16°25' ♉	☉-P
10/17/02	13S	22°56' ♈	☽-T
10/31/02	13N	6°59' ♏	☉-P
03/29/03	13S	7°11' ♈	☉-A
04/12/03	13N	20°56' ♎	☽-P
09/21/03	14N	27°01' ♍	☉-T
10/06/03	14S	12°11' ♈	☽-P
03/03/04	14N	11°07' ♍	☽-A
03/17/04	14S	26°13' ♓	☉-A
03/31/04	14N	10°23' ♎	☽-A

09/09/04	15N	16°42' ♍	☉-T
09/24/04	15S	1°14' ♈	☽-A
02/19/05	15N	0°29' ♍	☽-P
03/06/05	15S	14°59' ♓	☉-A
08/15/05	16S	21°37' ♒	☽-P
08/30/05	16N	6°28' ♍	☉-T
02/09/06	16N	19°40' ♌	☽-T
02/23/06	16S	3°48' ♓	☉-P
07/21/06	17N-E	27°30' ♋	☉-P
08/04/06	17S	11°13' ♒	☽-T
08/20/06	17N	26°07' ♌	☉-P
01/14/07	17S	22°56' ♑	☉-T
01/29/07	17N	8°31' ♌	☽-P
07/10/07	18N	17°12' ♋	☉-A
07/25/07	18S	1°05' ♒	☽-P
01/03/08	18S	12°08' ♑	☉-T
01/18/08	18N	27°05' ♋	☽-A
06/14/08	19S	23°04' ♐	☽-A
06/28/08	19N	6°32' ♋	☉-A
07/13/08	19S	21°02' ♑	☽-A
12/07/08	19N	15°25' ♊	☽-A
12/23/08	19S	1°17' ♑	☉-A
06/04/09	1S	12°46' ♐	☽-T
06/17/09	1N	26°05' ♊	☉-T
11/27/09	1N	4°29' ♊	☽-T
12/12/09	1S	20°11' ♐	☉-P
05/09/10	2N-E	17°43' ♉	☉-T
05/24/10	2S	2°10' ♐	☽-T
11/02/10	2S	8°46' ♏	☉-P
11/17/10	2N	23°47' ♉	☽-T
04/28/11	3N	7°30' ♉	☉-T
05/13/11	3S	21°22' ♏	☽-A
10/22/11	3S	27°33' ♎	☉-A
11/06/11	3N	13°07' ♉	☽-A
04/01/12	4S	11°49' ♎	☽-P
04/17/12	4N	27°05' ♈	☉-A
09/26/12	4N	3°00' ♈	☽-P
10/10/12	4S	16°53' ♎	☉-T

Date	Series	Position	Eclipse
03/22/13	5S	1°16' ♎	☽-T
04/06/13	5N	16°19' ♈	☉-P
08/31/13	5S-E	7°48' ♍	☉-P
09/15/13	5N	22°03' ♓	☽-T
09/30/13	5S	6°25' ♎	☉-P
02/25/14	6N	5°33' ♓	☉-A
03/12/14	6S	20°46' ♍	☽-P
08/21/14	6S	27°35' ♌	☉-T
09/04/14	6N	11°11' ♓	☽-P
01/31/15	7S	10°14' ♌	☽-A
02/14/15	7N	24°25' ♒	☉-A
03/02/15	7S	10°06' ♍	☽-A
07/26/15	7N	2°25' ♒	☽-A
08/10/15	7S	17°12' ♌	☉-A
08/24/15	7N	00°37' ♓	☽-A
01/20/16	8S	28°58' ♋	☽-P
02/03/16	8N	13°31' ♒	☉-T
07/15/16	8N	22°20' ♑	☽-P
07/30/16	8S	6°34' ♌	☉-A
12/24/16	9N-E	2°44' ♑	☉-P
01/08/17	9S	17°29' ♋	☽-T
01/23/17	9N	2°45' ♒	☉-P
06/19/17	9S-E	27°39' ♊	☉-P
07/04/17	9N	12°18' ♑	☽-T
07/19/17	9S**	25°51' ♋	☉-P
12/14/17	10N	21°50' ♐	☉-A
12/28/17	10S	6°07' ♋	☽-T
06/08/18	10S	17°16' ♊	☉-T
06/24/18	10N	2°05' ♑	☽-P
12/03/18	11N	10°40' ♐	☉-A
12/17/18	11S	25°04' ♊	☽-A
05/15/19	11N	23°09' ♏	☽-A
05/29/19	11S	7°06' ♊	☉-T
11/07/19	12S	14°31' ♉	☽-P
11/22/19	12N	29°17' ♏	☉-A
05/03/20	12N	12°19' ♏	☽-T
05/18/20	12S	27°00' ♉	☉-P

10/27/20	13S	3°52' ♉	☽-T
11/10/20	13N	17°58' ♏	☉-P
04/08/21	13S	17°59' ♈	☉-A
04/22/21	13N	1°38' ♏	☽-T
10/01/21	14N	7°47' ♎	☉-T
10/16/21	14S	23°02' ♈	☽-P
03/13/22	14N	22°06' ♍	☽-A
03/28/22	14S	7°04' ♈	☉-A
04/11/22	14N	21°10' ♎	☽-A
09/21/22	15N	27°24' ♍	☉-T
10/01/22	15S	11°59' ♈	☽-A
03/03/23	15N	11°32' ♍	☽-P
03/17/23	15S	25°55' ♓	☉-A
08/26/23	16S	2°09' ♓	☽-P
09/10/23	16N	17°06' ♍	☉-T
02/20/24	16N	00°46' ♍	☽-T
03/05/24	16S	14°49' ♓	☉-P
07/31/24	17N-E	8°16' ♌	☉-P
08/14/24	17S	21°43' ♒	☽-T
08/30/24	17N	6°40' ♍	☉-P
01/24/25	17S	4°08' ♒	☉-T
02/08/25	17N	19°39' ♌	☽-P
07/20/25	18N	27°37' ♋	☉-A
08/04/25	18S	11°34' ♒	☽-P
01/14/26	18S	23°21' ♑	☉-T
01/28/26	18N	8°14' ♌	☽-A
06/25/26	19S	3°31' ♑	☽-A
07/09/26	19N	16°37' ♋	☉-A
07/25/26	19S	1°30' ♒	☽-A
12/19/26	19N	26°35' ♊	☽-A
01/03/27	19S	12°29' ♑	☉-A
06/15/27	1S	23°14' ♐	☽-T
06/29/27	1N	6°31' ♋	☉-T
12/08/27	1N	15°38' ♊	☽-T
12/24/27	1S	1°21' ♑	☉-P

Date		Degree	Type
05/19/28	2N-E	28°17' ♉	☉-T
06/03/28	2S	12°39' ♐	☽-T
06/17/28	2N**	26°22' ♊	☉-P
11/12/28	2S	19°46' ♏	☉-P
11/27/28	2N	4°54' ♊	☽-T
05/09/29	3N	18°07' ♉	☉-T
05/23/29	3S	1°53' ♐	☽-A
11/01/29	3S	8°35' ♏	☉-A
11/17/29	3N	24°10' ♉	☽-A
04/13/30	4S	22°35' ♎	☽-P
04/28/30	4N	7°45' ♉	☉-A
10/07/30	4N	13°47' ♈	☽-P
10/21/30	4S	27°46' ♎	☉-T
04/02/31	5S	12°07' ♎	☽-T
04/18/31	5N	27°03' ♈	☉-P
09/12/31	5S-E*	18°27' ♍	☉-P
09/26/31	5N	2°45' ♈	☽-T
10/11/31	5S	17°15' ♎	☉-P
03/07/32	6N	16°32' ♓	☉-A
03/22/32	6S	1°41' ♎	☽-P
08/31/32	6S	8°10' ♍	☉-T
09/14/32	6N	21°49' ♓	☽-P
02/10/33	7S	21°22' ♌	☽-A
02/24/33	7N	5°29' ♓	☉-A
03/12/33	7S	21°05' ♍	☽-A
08/05/33	7N	12°53' ♒	☽-A
08/21/33	7S	27°42' ♌	☉-A
09/04/33	7N	11°12' ♓	☽-A
01/30/34	8S	10°07' ♌	☽-P
02/14/34	8N	24°39' ♒	☉-T
07/26/34	8N	2°48' ♒	☽-P
08/10/34	8S	17°02' ♌	☉-A
01/05/35	9N-E*	13°57' ♑	☉-P
01/19/35	9S	28°39' ♋	☽-T
02/03/35	9N	13°56' ♒	☉-P
06/30/35	9S-E*	8°04' ♋	☉-P
07/16/35	9N	22°45' ♑	☽-T
07/30/35	9S	6°18' ♌	☉-P

12/25/35	10N	3°01' ♑	☉-A
01/08/36	10S	17°19' ♋	☽-T
06/19/36	10S	27°44' ♊	☉-T
07/04/36	10N	12°31' ♑	☽-P
12/13/36	11N	21°49' ♐	☉-A
12/28/36	11S	6°16' ♋	☽-A
05/25/37	11N	3°40' ♐	☽-A
06/08/37	11S	17°36' ♊	☉-T
11/18/37	12S	25°35' ♉	☽-P
12/02/37	12N	10°23' ♐	☉-A
05/14/38	12N	22°54' ♏	☽-T
05/29/38	12S	7°32' ♊	☉-T
11/07/38	13S	14°51' ♉	☽-T
11/22/38	13N	29°02' ♏	☉-P
04/19/39	13S	28°44' ♈	☉-A
05/03/39	13N	12°18' ♏	☽-T
10/12/39	14N	18°37' ♎	☉-T
10/28/39	14S	3°57' ♉	☽-P
03/23/40	14N	3°01' ♎	☽-A
04/07/40	14S	17°52' ♈	☉-A
04/22/40	14N	1°54' ♏	☽-A
10/01/40	15N	8°11' ♎	☉-T
10/16/40	15S	22°49' ♈	☽-A
03/13/41	15N	22°31' ♍	☽-P
03/27/41	15S	7°46' ♈	☉-A
09/05/41	16S	12°45' ♓	☽-P
09/21/41	16N	27°48' ♍	☉-T
03/03/42	16N	11°48' ♍	☽-T
03/16/42	16S	25°46' ♓	☉-P
08/12/42	17N-E*	18°45' ♌	☉-P
08/26/42	17S	2°17' ♓	☽-T
09/10/42	17N	17°18' ♍	☉-P
02/04/43	17S	15°17' ♒	☉-T
02/20/43	17N	00°43' ♍	☽-P

08/01/43	18N	8°03' ♌	☉-A
08/15/43	18S	22°05' ♒	☽-P
01/25/44	18S	4°33' ♒	☉-T
02/09/44	18N	19°21' ♌	☽-A
07/06/44	19S	13°58' ♑	☽-A
07/20/44	19N	27°22' ♋	☉-A
08/04/44	19S	11°59' ♒	☽-A
12/29/44	19N	7°47' ♋	☽-A
01/14/45	19S	23°41' ♑	☉-A
06/25/45	1S	3°40' ♑	☽-P
07/09/45	1N	16°57' ♋	☉-T
12/19/45	1N	26°50' ♊	☽-T
01/03/46	1S	12°33' ♑	☉-P
05/30/46	2N-E	8°49' ♊	☉-P
06/14/46	2S	23°05' ♐	☽-T
06/29/46	2N	6°49' ♋	☉-P
11/23/46	2S	00°50' ♐	☉-P
12/08/46	2N	16°03' ♊	☽-T
05/20/47	3N	28°42' ♉	☉-T
06/03/47	3S	12°22' ♐	☽-P
11/12/47	3S	19°36' ♏	☉-A
11/28/47	3N	5°16' ♊	☽-A
04/23/48	4S	3°18' ♏	☽-P
05/09/48	4N	18°22' ♉	☉-A
10/18/48	4N	24°37' ♈	☽-A
11/01/48	4S	8°44' ♏	☉-T
04/13/49	5S	22°54' ♎	☽-T
04/28/49	5N	7°42' ♉	☉-P
10/07/49	5N	13°30' ♈	☽-T
10/21/49	5S	28°09' ♎	☉-P
03/18/50	6N	27°28' ♓	☉-A
04/02/50	6S	12°32' ♎	☽-T
09/12/50	6S	18°48' ♍	☉-T
09/26/50	6N	2°31' ♈	☽-T

Date	Series	Longitude		Type
02/21/51	7S	2°26'	♍	☽-A
03/07/51	7N	16°29'	♓	☉-A
03/23/51	7S	2°00'	♎	☽-A
08/17/51	7N	23°25'	♒	☽-A
09/01/51	7S	8°16'	♍	☉-A
09/15/51	7N	21°52'	♓	☽-A
02/11/52	8S	21°14'	♌	☽-P
02/25/52	8N	5°43'	♓	☉-T
08/05/52	8N	13°17'	♒	☽-P
08/20/52	8S	27°31'	♌	☉-A
01/29/53	9S	9°48'	♌	☽-T
02/14/53	9N	25°03'	♒	☉-P
07/11/53	9S-E	18°30'	♋	☉-P
07/26/53	9N	3°12'	♒	☽-T
08/09/53	9S	16°45'	♌	☉-P
01/05/54	10N	14°13'	♑	☉-A
01/19/54	10S	28°30'	♋	☽-T
06/30/54	10S	8°10'	♋	☉-T
07/16/54	10N	22°57'	♑	☽-P
12/25/54	11N	2°59'	♑	☉-A
01/08/55	11S	17°28'	♋	☽-A
06/05/55	11N	14°08'	♐	☽-A
06/20/55	11S	28°05'	♊	☉-T
11/29/55	12S	6°42'	♊	☽-P
12/14/55	12N	21°31'	♐	☉-A
05/24/56	12N	3°25'	♐	☽-P
06/08/56	12S	18°02'	♊	☉-T
11/18/56	13S	25°55'	♉	☽-T
12/02/56	13N	10°09'	♐	☉-P
04/29/57	13S	9°23'	♉	☉-T
05/13/57	13N	22°52'	♏	☽-T
10/23/57	14N	29°31'	♎	☉-P
11/07/57	14S	14°55'	♉	☽-T
04/04/58	14N	13°52'	♎	☽-A
04/19/58	14S	28°34'	♈	☉-A
05/03/58	14N	12°34'	♏	☽-P

10/12/58	15N	19°01' ♎	☉-T
10/27/58	15S	3°43' ♉	☽-A
03/24/59	15N	3°26' ♎	☽-P
04/08/59	15S	17°34' ♈	☉-A
09/17/59	16S	23°24' ♓	☽-A
10/02/59	16N	8°34' ♎	☉-T
03/13/60	16N	22°47' ♍	☽-T
03/27/60	16S	6°39' ♈	☉-P
09/05/60	17S	12°53' ♓	☽-T
09/20/60	17N	27°58' ♍	☉-P
02/15/61	17S	26°25' ♒	☉-T
03/02/61	17N	11°45' ♍	☽-P
08/11/61	18N	18°31' ♌	☉-A
08/26/61	18S	2°39' ♓	☽-T
02/05/62	18S	15°43' ♒	☉-T
02/19/62	18N	00°25' ♍	☽-A
07/17/62	19S	24°25' ♑	☽-A
07/31/62	19N	7°49' ♌	☉-A
08/15/62	19S	22°30' ♒	☽-A
01/09/63	19N	18°59' ♋	☽-A
01/25/63	19S	4°52' ♒	☉-A
07/06/63	1S	14°06' ♑	☽-P
07/20/63	1N	27°24' ♋	☉-T
12/30/63	1N	8°01' ♋	☽-T
01/14/64	1S	23°43' ♑	☉-P
06/10/64	2N-E	19°19' ♊	☉-P
06/25/64	2S	3°30' ♑	☽-T
07/09/64	2N	17°16' ♋	☉-P
12/04/64	2S	11°56' ♐	☉-P
12/19/64	2N	27°14' ♊	☽-T
05/30/65	3N	9°13' ♊	☉-T
06/14/65	3S	22°48' ♐	☽-P
11/23/65	3S	00°40' ♐	☉-A
12/08/65	3N	16°25' ♊	☽-A
05/04/66	4S	13°56' ♏	☽-A
05/20/66	4N	28°55' ♉	☉-A
10/29/66	4N	5°32' ♉	☽-A
11/12/66	4S	19°45' ♏	☉-T

04/24/67	5S	3°37' ♏	☽-T
05/09/67	5N	18°18' ♉	☉-P
10/18/67	5N	24°21' ♈	☽-T
11/02/67	5S	9°07' ♏	☉-T
03/28/68	6N	8°19' ♈	☉-P
04/13/68	6S	23°23' ♎	☽-T
09/22/68	6S	29°30' ♍	☉-T
10/06/68	6N	13°17' ♈	☽-T
03/18/69	7N	27°25' ♓	☉-A
04/02/69	7S	12°51' ♎	☽-A
08/27/69	7N	3°58' ♓	☽-A
09/11/69	7S	18°53' ♍	☉-A
09/25/69	7N	2°35' ♈	☽-A
02/21/70	8S	2°18' ♍	☽-P
03/07/70	8N	16°44' ♓	☉-T
08/17/70	8N	23°49' ♒	☽-P
08/31/70	8S	8°04' ♍	☉-A
09/15/70	8N	22°12' ♓	☽-A
02/10/71	9S	20°55' ♌	☽-T
02/25/71	9N	6°09' ♓	☉-P
07/22/71	9S-E*	28°56' ♋	☉-P
08/06/71	9N	13°41' ♒	☽-T
08/20/71	9S	27°15' ♌	☉-P
01/16/72	10N	25°25' ♑	☉-A
01/30/72	10S	9°39' ♌	☽-T
07/10/72	10S	18°37' ♋	☉-T
07/26/72	10N	3°24' ♒	☽-P
01/04/73	11N	14°10' ♑	☉-A
01/18/73	11S	28°40' ♋	☽-A
06/15/73	11N	24°35' ♐	☽-A
06/30/73	11S	8°32' ♋	☉-T
07/15/73	11N	22°51' ♑	☽-A
12/10/73	12S	17°51' ♊	☽-P
12/24/73	12N	2°40' ♑	☉-A
06/04/74	12N	13°54' ♐	☽-P
06/20/74	12S	28°30' ♊	☉-T

11/29/74	13S	7°01' ♊	☽-T
12/13/74	13N	21°17' ♐	☉-P
05/11/75	13S	19°59' ♉	☉-P
05/25/75	13N	3°25' ♐	☽-T
11/03/75	14N	10°29' ♏	☉-P
11/18/75	14S	25°58' ♉	☽-T
04/29/76	14S	9°13' ♉	☉-A
05/13/76	14N	23°10' ♏	☽-P
10/23/76	15N	29°55' ♎	☉-T
11/06/76	15S	14°41' ♉	☽-A
04/04/77	15N	14°17' ♎	☽-P
04/18/77	15S	28°17' ♈	☉-A
09/27/77	16S	4°07' ♈	☽-A
10/12/77	16N	19°24' ♎	☉-T
03/24/78	16N	3°40' ♎	☽-T
04/07/78	16S	17°27' ♈	☉-P
09/16/78	17S	23°33' ♓	☽-T
10/02/78	17N	8°43' ♎	☉-P
02/26/79	17S	7°29' ♓	☉-T
03/13/79	17N	22°42' ♍	☽-P
08/22/79	18N	29°01' ♌	☉-T
09/06/79	18S	13°16' ♓	☽-T
02/16/80	18S	26°50' ♒	☉-T
03/01/80	18N	11°26' ♍	☽-A
07/27/80	19S	4°52' ♒	☽-A
08/10/80	19N	18°17' ♌	☉-A
08/26/80	19S	3°03' ♓	☽-A
01/20/81	19N	00°10' ♌	☽-A
02/04/81	19S	16°02' ♒	☉-A
07/17/81	1S	24°31' ♑	☽-P
07/31/81	1N	7°51' ♌	☉-T
01/09/82	1N	19°14' ♋	☽-T
01/25/82	1S	4°54' ♒	☉-P
06/21/82	2N-E	29°47' ♊	☉-P
07/06/82	2S	13°55' ♑	☽-T
07/20/82	2N	27°43' ♋	☉-P
12/15/82	2S	23°04' ♐	☉-P
12/30/82	2N	8°27' ♋	☽-T

06/11/83	3N	19°43' ♊	☉-T
06/25/83	3S	3°14' ♑	☽-P
12/04/83	3S	11°47' ♐	☉-A
12/20/83	3N	27°36' ♊	☽-A
05/15/84	4S	24°31' ♏	☽-A
05/30/84	4N	9°26' ♊	☉-A
06/13/84	4S	22°45' ♐	☽-A
11/08/84	4N	16°30' ♉	☽-A
11/22/84	4S	00°50' ♐	☉-T
05/04/85	5S	14°17' ♏	☽-T
05/19/85	5N	28°50' ♉	☉-P
10/28/85	5N	5°15' ♉	☽-T
11/12/85	5S	20°09' ♏	☉-T
04/09/86	6N	19°06' ♈	☉-P
04/24/86	6S	4°03' ♏	☽-T
10/03/86	6S	10°16' ♎	☉-T
10/17/86	6N	24°07' ♈	☽-T
03/29/87	7N	8°18' ♈	☉-A
04/14/87	7S	23°38' ♎	☽-A
09/23/87	7S	29°34' ♍	☉-A
10/07/87	7N	13°22' ♈	☽-P
03/03/88	8S	13°18' ♍	☽-P
03/18/88	8N	27°42' ♓	☉-T
08/27/88	8N	4°23' ♓	☽-P
09/11/88	8S	18°40' ♍	☉-A
02/20/89	9S	1°59' ♍	☽-T
03/07/89	9N	17°10' ♓	☉-P
08/17/89	9N	24°12' ♒	☽-T
08/31/89	9S	7°48' ♍	☉-P
01/26/90	10N	6°35' ♒	☉-A
02/09/90	10S	20°47' ♌	☽-T
07/22/90	10S	29°04' ♋	☉-T
08/06/90	10N	13°52' ♒	☽-P
01/15/91	11N	25°20' ♑	☉-A
01/30/91	11S	9°51' ♌	☽-A
06/27/91	11N	5°00' ♑	☽-A
07/11/91	11S	18°59' ♋	☉-T
07/26/91	11N	3°16' ♒	☽-A

Date	Series	Position	Type
12/21/91	12S	29°03' ♊	☽-P
01/04/92	12N	13°51' ♑	☉-A
06/15/92	12N	24°20' ♐	☽-P
06/30/92	12S	8°57' ♋	☉-T
12/09/92	13S	18°10' ♊	☽-T
12/24/92	13N	2°28' ♑	☉-P
05/21/93	13S	00°31' ♊	☉-P
06/04/93	13N	13°55' ♐	☽-T
11/13/93	14N	21°32' ♏	☉-P
11/29/93	14S	7°03' ♊	☽-T
05/10/94	14S	19°48' ♉	☉-A
05/25/94	14N	3°43' ♐	☽-P
11/03/94	15N	10°54' ♏	☉-T
11/18/94	15S	25°42' ♉	☽-A
04/15/95	15N	25°04' ♎	☽-P
04/29/95	15S	8°56' ♉	☉-A
10/08/95	16S	14°54' ♈	☽-A
10/24/95	16N	00°18' ♏	☉-T
04/04/96	16N	14°31' ♎	☽-T
04/17/96	16S	28°12' ♈	☉-P
09/27/96	17S	4°17' ♈	☽-T
10/12/96	17N	19°32' ♎	☉-P
03/09/97	17S	18°31' ♓	☉-T
03/24/97	17N	3°35' ♎	☽-P
09/01/97	18N	9°34' ♍	☉-P
09/16/97	18S	23°56' ♓	☽-T
02/26/98	18S	7°55' ♓	☉-T
03/13/98	18N	22°24' ♍	☽-A
08/08/98	19S	15°21' ♒	☽-A
08/22/98	19N	28°48' ♌	☉-A
09/06/98	19S	13°40' ♓	☽-A
01/31/99	19N	11°20' ♌	☽-A
02/16/99	19S	27°08' ♒	☉-A
07/28/99	1S	4°58' ♒	☽-P
08/11/99	1N	18°21' ♌	☉-T

*Final eclipse in series.   **Initial eclipse in series.

KEY: N = ☊; S = ☋; E = The earlier starting of two concurrently operating members of the same series; A = Lunar appulse or annular solar eclipse; P = Partial eclipse; T = Total eclipse.

BIBLIOGRAPHY

Bartolet, Sam. *Eclipses and Lunations in Astrology.* Tempe, AZ: American Federation of Astrologers.

Devore, Nicholas. *Encyclopedia of Astrology.* Totowa, NJ: Littlefield, Adams and Co., 1976.

Jansky, Robert. "Using Solar Eclipses in Forecasting." *American Federation of Astrologers Bulletin*, Vol. 41, No. 9 (September 1979), pp. 13-17.

Jansky, Robert Carl. *Interpreting the Eclipses.* Van Nuys, CA: Astro-analytics Publications, 1977.

Lineman, Rose. "A Look at Lunar Eclipses." *American Federation of Astrologers Bulletin*, Vol. 43, No. 3 (March 1981) pp. 84, 85, 87.

Eclipses: Astrological Guideposts. Tempe, AZ: American Federation of Astrologers, 1984.

Lineman, Rose, and Jan Popelka. *Compendium of Astrology.* Gloucester, MA: Para Research, Inc., 1984.

INDEX

Decanate (see Decan)
Deneb Algedi, 9
Descendant
    aspects with lunar eclipse, (see also names of aspects), 103-106
    aspects with solar eclipse, (see also names of aspects), 71-74
Dispositor, 77, 113-114, 116
Duad, 2, 13, 18, 114
    eighth of Libra, 5
    eleventh
        of Aries, 4
        of Cancer, 8
        of Gemini, 3
        of Leo, 4
        of Pisces, 8
    fifth
        of Aries, 7
        of Cancer, 11
        of Gemini, 4, 12
        of Taurus, 3, 8
        of Virgo, 10
    first, 2
        of Taurus, 3
    ninth
        of Aquarius, 12
        of Cancer, 5, 12
        of Leo, 10
        of Libra, 4
        of Pisces, 6
    second of Virgo, 12
    seventh
        of Leo, 7, 9
        of Libra, 6
        of Taurus, 10
    sixth of Capricorn, 2
    tenth
        of Aquarius, 9
        of Gemini, 11
    third
        of Cancer, 3, 6, 8
        of Gemini, 6